Life Of Richard Brinsley Sheridan

Lloyd Charles Sanders

LIFE

OF

RICHARD BRINSLEY SHERIDAN

BY

LLOYD C. SANDERS.

————————

LONDON:

WALTER SCOTT, 24 WARWICK LANE.

NEW YORK: 3 EAST 14TH STREET,
AND' MELBOURNE.

CONTENTS.

CHAPTER I.

CHAPTER VII.

CHAPTER VIII.

CHAPTER IX.

LIFE OF SHERIDAN.

CHAPTER I.

THE Anglo-Irish family of Sheridan possessed in a marked degree the dominant characteristics of their race—ability, buoyancy, and thriftlessness. Among Swift's Irish friends none is so interesting as Dr. Thomas Sheridan, the dramatist's grandfather. He was an accomplished scholar, and a good schoolmaster; excellent company—Lord Orrery describes him as a punster, a quibbler, a fiddler, and a wit—but hopelessly improvident and hopelessly devoid of tact, though assuredly not of tenderness. He was one of the few men whom Swift seems to have really esteemed, though the Dean's calculating friendship but poorly returned the wealth of affection bestowed on him by the open-hearted Irishman. In justice to Swift, however, it should be pointed out that Dr. Sheridan was one of those persons for whom it is well-nigh impossible to obtain anything. He was appointed one of the chaplains to the Lord Lieutenant, but was promptly struck off the list for a very adequate reason. It fell to his lot to preach at Cork on the king's birthday, and what must he do but select the text, "Sufficient unto the day is the evil thereof"? "Too much advertency is not your talent," wrote Swift to him in mild rebuke, " or else you had fled from that text as from a rock. For as Don Quixote said to Sancho, ' What business had you to speak of a halter in a family where one of it was hanged?'" Sheridan bought a school at Cavan in 1735, whence he conducted a rollicking correspondence with Swift. But two years afterwards he sold the school for £400, and, as his friend briefly records, "spent the money, grew into disease, and died." George IV., on reading his correspondence with Swift, remarked to Croker how exactly his character corresponded with that of his brilliant grandson, and the parallel is tolerably obvious.

Dr. Sheridan's third son Thomas is a sufficiently familiar figure in the pages of Boswell, and may perhaps be briefly described as an ineffectual genius, whose great talents were spoilt by diffuseness and pedantry. At first an actor, he became a popular favourite at Dublin, and though hardly, as has been asserted, a rival of Garrick, trod the London boards with considerable credit, notably in the parts of Brutus and King John. As the manager of a Dublin theatre he did not win success, and became the victim of various theatrical conspiracies, but was fortunate enough to secure the anonymous advocacy, and win the hand, of the accomplished young authoress, Frances Chamberlaine. She was of good family, the granddaughter of an English baronet, and her father was a dignitary of the Irish Church. They were married in 1747, and their second son, Richard Brinsley Butler, was born at No. 12, Dorset Street, Dublin, on the 30th of October, 1751.[1]

The parents seem to have divided their time, with the exception of a professional visit to London, between the Irish capital and the meagre family estate at Quilca, until 1758, when they finally removed to England. Richard and his sister Alicia remained behind, and went first as day-scholars, and then as boarders, to Mr. Whyte's, of Grafton Street, Dublin, who afterwards taught Moore, Sheridan's biographer. About eighteen months later they followed their parents across the Channel, and found the house in Henrietta Street, Covent Garden, the centre of a literary society, of which Samuel Richardson and Dr. Johnson were the most celebrated members. Mrs. Sheridan meanwhile was trying to keep the wolf from the door by writing her novel, "The Adventures of Miss Sidney Biddulph," a very remarkable specimen of the Richardsonian school of fiction, which won the cordial approbation of Lord North and Mr. Fox, while Dr. Johnson said of it that he knew not if she had a right, on moral principles, to make her characters suffer so much. A comedy entitled "The Discovery" followed, which was promptly accepted by Garrick, and which contained in Sir Anthony Branville one of his favourite parts. "The Dupe" however failed, owing to the indelicacy of some of its situations, or according to another story, through the cabals of the famous actress, Mrs. Clive.

[1] This is the date given by Mr. Chester in his notes to the "Registers in Westminster Abbey." Sheridan's biographers say vaguely that he was born in September.

The father was employed in acting, and in lecturing on
British education. His scheme was about equally com-
pounded of common sense and whim ; he saw the value
of professional training in youth, but he vastly over-
estimated the worth of oratory as a medium for bringing
up the young idea. He was also compiling a "Pro-
nouncing Dictionary of the English Language," and
received as an encouragement to his undertaking a
pension of £200 a year. "What ? " said Johnson,
"have they given *him* a pension? Then it is time for
me to give up mine." A quarrel naturally ensued, which
was never completely healed, though the Doctor made
more than one overture. The original cause of offence
was the more uncalled for, because it was owing to
Sheridan's influence with Wedderburne, to whom he had
given lessons in English pronunciation, that Dr. Johnson
owed his own pension. Nor is it fair to take seriously
his scathing speech. "Why, sir, Sherry is dull, naturally
dull, but it must have taken him a deal of pains to
become what he is. Such an excess of stupidity is not
in nature. . . . Besides, Sir, what influence can Mr.
Sheridan have upon the language of this great country
through his narrow exertions. It is burning a farthing
candle at Dover, to show light at Calais." Lexicographers
apparently do not always agree.

Affluence and the Sheridans dwelt far apart, and in
1764, the father, mother, and two daughters, influenced
partly by pecuniary considerations, partly by the state
of Mrs. Sheridan's health, retired to Blois. The
admirable woman—Dr. Parr termed her " quite celes-
tial "—had only time to write an Oriental tale " Nour-

jahad," and the second part of " Sidney Biddulph," when she died in August, 1766. Thus her son Dick never saw her again, for he had gone to Harrow in 1762, where he was placed under the care of his father's acquaintance, Dr. Sumner. His schooldays do not call for any especial comment. Both masters and boys liked him, and though he was apparently idle, and Dr. Parr in vain attempted to extract from him some signs of that superior intelligence which he was known to possess, yet it is probable that he managed to pick up a fair amount of scholarship. Indeed he had already entered into a literary partnership with a schoolfellow called Halhed, and the pair translated the Seventh Idyl and many of the lesser poems of Theocritus, a performance which in itself is sufficient to prove that Dr. Parr's knowledge of his pupil was superficial. We gather, too, that the future orator was chosen to recite a Greek speech, which his budding extravagance suggested to him would be most appropriately delivered in the uniform of a British general officer. He had also developed the taste for practical jokes which distinguished him through life; his myrmidons robbed apple-orchards for him, and the thefts could never be traced to their instigator.

Sheridan left Harrow in his seventeenth year, and lived with his father and elder brother Charles in Frith Street, Soho. Want of means alone would probably have prevented his being sent to the University, but it does not follow, as is sometimes asserted, that old Sheridan was careless of his son's future. He was at this time maturing his educational scheme, and in 1769

it was published with a letter to the king, in which the
author offered to devote his life to the cause, on the
receipt of a sufficient pension to enable him to abandon
the theatre. Visions of an academy in which he would
be the guiding spirit, and his sons the executive, floated
before the gaze of this sanguine Irishman, and with that
view he instructed them daily in elocution. At the same
time they received lessons in Latin and mathematics from
a Mr. Ker, while the remainder of a polite education
was acquired at Angelo's riding-school. The royal ear,
however, was invoked in vain, and old Sheridan, nothing
daunted, retired in 1771—not 1770, as stated by Moore
in his "Life of Sheridan"—to Bath, where he worked
away at his dictionary, which ultimately appeared in
1780. "What, Sir," asked Dr. Johnson, "entitled
Sheridan to fix the pronunciation of English ? "

Meantime the literary association with Halhed had
been resumed, young Sheridan being perhaps doubtful
of the ultimate success of his father's schemes, and
anxious to make a living by his pen. Their first essay
was a farce called "Jupiter," which contains some clever
dialogue, but is chiefly remarkable for being thrown into
the form of a rehearsal, and thus an anticipation of
"The Critic." Another attempt, for which Sheridan
alone was responsible, was a dramatic sketch founded on
the "Vicar of Wakefield." A periodical paper entitled
Herman's Miscellany was then projected, but never
proceeded beyond the first number, written by Sheridan,
while a "Collection of Occasional Poems," and a volume
of "Crazy Tales," seem to have perished in embryo. In
fact, the only production which saw the light was a verse

translation of the Epistles of an obscure Greek author named Aristænetus, which was published in August, 1771. The MS. was due in March, but owing to Sheridan's laziness, and possibly owing to his limited knowledge of Greek—though he conscientiously supplemented his deficiencies by the aid of a grammar—it does not appear to have reached the publisher Wilkie until May. Taken as a whole the performance was by no means discreditable—in fact, Sheridan had little cause to be ashamed of any of his early efforts—but it was far from proving a pecuniary success. A report that the volume was making a stir in London, and had been attributed to Dr. Johnson, was followed by its comparative failure. It succeeded somehow or other in struggling into a second edition, but the collaborators were wise enough not to venture on a second instalment.

Though the data are few, it is probable that young Sheridan had little difficulty in making his way in the easy society of the queen of watering-places. The place must have been, however, an unwholesome home for so precocious a boy, and to his vagrant youth, combined with the early death of his mother, must be attributed much of that absence of self-restraint which operated so disastrously upon his manhood and old age. His figure was tall and graceful; of his face Byron wrote that, even in his decline, "the upper part was that of a god—a forehead most expansive, an eye of peculiar brilliancy and fire"; he shone in conversation, and could turn out a very pretty copy of verses on the spur of the moment. The last quality must have made him popular among the frequenters of Lady Miller's house at Bath Easton, where according to Horace Walpole, "all the flux of quality contended for prizes gained for rhymes and themes ; a Roman vase, dressed with pink ribbons and myrtle, received the poetry which was drawn out at each festival"; the victor knelt and kissed the hand of Lady Miller, who crowned him with a wreath. A more capti-vating person, Lady Margaret Fordyce, sister of Lady Anne Lindsay, the writer of "Auld Robin Grey," was celebrated by him in the well-known passage :—

> . . : "Mark'd you her cheek of rosy hue ?
> Mark'd you her eye of sparkling blue ?
> That eye, in liquid circles moving ;
> That cheek abashed at Man's approving ;
> The *one* Love's arrows darting round ;
> The *other* blushing at the wound :
> Did she not speak, did she not move,
> Now *Pallas*—now the Queen of Love !

The lines occur in a poem called "Clio's Protest; or the Picture Varnished," an answer to some verses de-scriptive of the beauties of Bath by General Fitzpatrick, subsequently one of Sheridan's intimates, which were entitled "The Bath Picture." "Clio's Protest" also contained the familiar couplet—

> "You write with ease to show your breeding,
> But *easy writing's* vile *hard* reading."

In another effusion, styled "A Panegyric to the Ridotto," given when the new Assembly Rooms were opened on the 30th of September, 1771, he satirized the tradespeople of Bath, and their undignified rush towards the supper-room. Timothy Screw, a waiter, is supposed to un-

burden his mind at their expense to his brother Henry,
a waiter at aristocratic Almack's.

> " But here I must mention the best thing of all,
> And what I'm informed ever marks a *Bath* ball,
> The variety 'tis which so reign'd in the crew,
> That turn where one would the classes were new :
> For here no dull level of rank and degrees,
> No uniform mode, that shows all are at ease ;
> But like a chess table, part black and part white,
> 'Twas a delicate chequer of *low* and *polite.*
>
>   .   .   .   .   .
>
> Not less among you was the medley, ye fair ;
> I believe there *were* some besides Quality there :
> Miss Spiggot, Miss Brussels, Miss Tape, and Miss Sockct,
> Miss Trinket, and aunt, with her leathern pocket ;
> With good Mrs. Soaker, who made her old chin go
> For hours, hobnobbing with Mrs. Syringo."

Among those who frequented Bath for professional
purposes were Mr. Linley, the composer, and his family,
" a nest of nightingales." The eldest daughter was
known as the Maid of Bath, and her beauty and exquisite
voice had already gathered round her a numerous band
of admirers, some of whom she was compelled, from her
position as a public singer, to treat with more ceremony
than they deserved. She was barely seventeen, but had
already had several offers of marriage, amongst others
from an elderly and wealthy gentleman of Wiltshire
named Long. Her parents naturally wished for the
marriage, but she told Mr. Long that she could never
be happy with him, and the good old man took upon
himself the responsibility of breaking off the alliance,
and even indemnified Mr. Linley, who was proceeding

to bring the matter into court, by settling £3,000 upon his daughter. Among those who entertained honourable designs were Halhed and Charles Sheridan ; of her unworthy lovers the most pertinacious was Mr. Mathews, a married man of fortune. It appears that the elders of the Sheridan and Linley families had already become acquainted, through Mrs. Sheridan having taken some singing lessons from Mr. Linley in 1764 ; and when the fathers met again at Bath, a close friendship was formed between their daughters, which the Sheridan boys naturally turned to their own account. Of the exact course of events it would be difficult, even if it were worth while, to give the history, since the long letter, purporting to be by Miss Linley, and written in Lydia Languish's best manner, upon which biographers commonly rely, has been denounced by Sheridan's granddaughter Mrs. Norton, as a clumsy forgery.[1] But it is clear that Richard Sheridan easily disposed of the claims of Halhed, absent at Oxford, and of the solemn Charles. His muse ably seconded his efforts by the pretty verses beginning—

> " Dry be that tear, my gentlest love,
> Be hush'd that struggling sigh. "

Halhed retired to India, Charles to a farmhouse near Bath, whence he wrote to Miss Linley a letter of farewell.

[1] A collection of letters, purporting to have been written by Miss Linley after her marriage with Sheridan, was published in *The English Illustrated Magazine* in 1884. As their authenticity appears to be decidedly doubtful, it is possible that they were concocted by the same hand that wrote the letter alluded to in the text.

Mathews alone held the field against Sheridan, and the romantic imagination of the latter suggested an elopement as the best means of furthering his own ends, and foiling those of his rival. With his sister's connivance the lovers fled to London, thence to Dunkirk, with money borrowed from a friend of the family upon the representation that Miss Linley was a rich heiress, with whom Sheridan was eloping. A secret marriage of a somewhat perfunctory nature was accomplished at Calais, and they proceeded to Lisle, where Miss Linley, as she must still be called, retired into a convent, until the arrival of her father who, tolerant, practical man, brought her back to England to fulfil her engagements.

The second act of the comedy begins with a violent libel upon Sheridan by Mathews in *The Bath Chronicle,* and then indeed the gossips of Bath had good cause to swear with Bob Acres by "Odds hilts and blades, odds flints, pans and triggers." There were two so-called duels—the first a scuffle in a London tavern, after which Mathews was compelled to apologize; the second a scuffle near Bath, in which Sheridan was wounded. If Sheridan's own account may be accepted, Mathews showed great cowardice in the first duel, but had much the better of the second, though Sheridan, who was wounded while the pair were rolling together on the ground, declined to beg his life. The young man's wrath seems, in fact, to have got the better of his science, and blood and ink were spilt in about equal quantities. In the last scene Miss Linley rushes on with the passionate exclamation, "My husband, my husband!" and the curtain falls upon a very effective situation.

In the third act, however, the interest begins to flag. Sheridan retired to Farm Hill near Waltham Abbey, and the paper warfare continued, a third duel being at one time in prospect. It was quite characteristic of him that he should have requested Woodfall to reprint in *The Morning Advertiser* a calumnious account of his conduct which had appeared in one of the Bath papers, so as to give him an opportunity of contradicting it, and then, from indolence, have omitted to send the counterblast. Meantime, old Sheridan would not hear of the marriage, and all communications were intercepted, while the appearance of Miss Linley in the oratorios at Covent Garden caused a fresh swarm of admirers to gather round her, and inflicted upon her husband *de jure*, if not *de facto*, those torments of groundless jealousy which, according to a not very tenable theory, he afterwards described in the character of Faulkland. Moore informs us that his nimble wit contrived many stratagems for the purpose of exchanging a few words with her, and that he more than once disguised himself as a hackney coachman, and drove her home from the theatre. Mr. Linley in the end proved less obdurate than Sheridan's father, and, the first ceremony being regarded as too informal, the lovers were married by license on April 13, 1773. The summer and autumn were spent in a cottage at East Burnham, and it was during a temporary absence that Sheridan wrote the lines which, in their perfected form, were one of the most popular songs in "The Duenna" :—

" What bard, O Time, discover,
With wings first made thee move?

Ah ! sure it was some lover
Who ne'er had left his love !
For who that once did prove
The pangs that absence brings,
Though but one day
He were away,
Could picture thee with wings !"

CHAPTER II.

EARLY in 1774 Sheridan and his wife proceeded to set up house in Orchard Street, Portman Square. No assistance was forthcoming from old Sheridan, who still harboured resentment against his son; but Mr. Linley supplied the furniture, and for ready money they had Mr. Long's three thousand pounds. The sum must have seemed an El Dorado to them, and they probably had little scruple about living on capital. An obvious source of income was Mrs. Sheridan's voice, but Sheridan at once rejected all thoughts of allowing her to perform in public, even though Lord North, the Chancellor of Oxford University, was reported as having said that her appearance there would be regarded as the highest compliment. Dr. Johnson warmly approved Sheridan's determination not to live upon his wife, and there can be no doubt that a manly sense of independence, not a weak compliance with social prejudices, was his actuating motive. It is probable, however, that the young couple at first intended to derive an income from a series of private entertainments, given in conjunction with the Linleys. At least there in a remarkably business-like tone in the following advertisement, which appeared in *The Morning Post* of February 4, 1774 :—

"Sheridan has taken a house in Orchard Street, Oxford Street, where he proposes, if his wife recovers, to give concerts twice a week to the nobility. Mrs. Sheridan has refused 1,200 guineas for twelve months at the Pantheon, 1,000 guineas for the Oratorios, and 1,000 for Gardiner's concert."

But the idea, a distinctly sensible one, seems to have been dropped. For we are assured by Sheridan's niece, Miss Lefanu, in her "Memoirs of Mrs. Frances Sheridan," that the concerts were given gratuitously, as a return for hospitalities received. The story is that the Sheridans took society by storm, sending out invitations and giving entertainments on equal terms to persons of distinction; and that when Sheridan was scolded for living beyond his means, he replied, "My dear Sir, these *are* my means." · Like most Sheridaniana, the anecdote probably contains more fable than fact; indeed, there is distinct evidence that the gifted pair found the ascent to Olympus by no means unencumbered by obstacles. Moore records that there was some hesitation before Devonshire House opened its doors to them, and so late as 1785 we find Mr. Windham recording in his diary that he had spent the morning with Mrs. Legge, and that their chief topic of conversation was the reasons for and against being acquainted with Mrs. Sheridan. In this instance it is not uncharitable to surmise that the lady was for the prosecution, the gentleman for the defence, and it is to be hoped that the former was effectually reduced to silence. But the entry conclusively proves that the Sheridans, like most ambitious people of similar antecedents, were at first rather in society than of it, and had to endure a considerable period of probation below the salt before they were finally promoted to a footing of equality.

Meanwhile Sheridan was looking about for a livelihood. He had been entered a student of the Middle Temple, but for a person in his situation it would have been an obvious absurdity to devote himself to a profession the income from which was certain to be remote, and might possibly never come at all. Literature afforded brighter prospects, and in November, 1774, he wrote to Mr. Linley that he was very seriously at work on a book, which he was sending to the press. Whatever the work in question may have been, it never emerged from the printer's hands. Moore is inclined to identify it with an " Essay on the Letters of Lord Chesterfield," of which he found a part of the rough copy among Sheridan's papers, and as those famous Letters had only recently appeared the subject was undoubtedly tempting. Of the fragments given by Moore, one is interesting as admitting us to the secret of Sheridan's habits of intellectual labour :—

" His [Lord Chesterfield's] directions for constant employment entirely ill-founded—a wise man is formed more by the action of his own thoughts than by continually feeding it. ' Hurry,' he says, ' from play to study ; never be doing nothing.' I say, ' Frequently be unemployed ; sit and think.' There are on every subject but a few leading and fixed ideas ; their tracks may be traced by your own genius as well as by reading."

But essays and pamphlets were certainly not the main

objects of his literary ambition. A successful drama is far
more lucrative than a successful book, and Sheridan had an
hereditary connection with the stage. His father was a
well-known actor and manager, his mother had been the
author of a highly successful play. He had, therefore,
already been collecting materials for "a scene or two,"
as he wrote to his father-in-law, "which I believe you
have seen in an odd act of a little farce." When Mr.
Harris, the manager of Covent Garden, asked him to
write a comedy, Sheridan answered his request by
producing " The Rivals."

The play was written in something like six weeks, and
as to its genesis there is some curious information in the
author's preface to the published edition :—

" Hurry in writing," he says, " has long been exploded as an
excuse for an author—however, in the dramatic line, it may happen
that both an author and a manager may wish to fill a chasm in the
entertainment of the public with a hastiness not altogether culpable.
The season was advanced when I first put the play into Mr.
Harris's hands ; it was at that time at least double the length of
any acting comedy. I profited by his judgment and experience in
curtailing of it, till, I believe, his feeling for the vanity of a young
author got the better of his desire for correctness, and he left many
excrescences remaining, because he had assisted in pruning so many
more."

In consequence of Mr. Harris's kind-heartedness,
when the play was produced on January 17, 1775, it was
still by far too long. Added to this the character of Sir
Lucius O'Trigger was apparently considered an offensive
reflection upon Irish peculiarities, and its exponent
Mr. Lee failed lamentably, in consequence of hostile
demonstrations from the Hibernian portion of the

audience, who were probably present in force to support their young fellow-countryman.[1] After a second trial, the play was judiciously withdrawn, to escape perpetual damnation, and submitted to considerable condensation. A new Sir Lucius was procured in the shape of Larry Clinch, an Irish friend of the elder Sheridan's, who did ample justice to the part. Further, Sheridan substituted for the original prologue—a somewhat flat dialogue between a serjeant-at-law, counsel for the poet, and an attorney—a new prologue, spoken by Mrs. Bulkley, the Julia of the play. The actress pointed to the figure of Comedy at the side of the stage, and told the audience to

> " Look on her well—does she seem form'd to teach ?
> Should you *expect* to hear this lady—preach ?
> Is gray experience suited to her youth,
> Do solemn sentiments become that mouth ?
> Bid her be grave, those lips would rebel prove
> To every theme that slanders mirth or love.
> Yet, thus adorned with every graceful art,
> To charm the fancy and to reach the heart,
> Must we displease her ? and instead advance
> The goddess of the woful countenance ?—
> The Sentimental Muse—Her emblems view—
> The ' Pilgrim's Progress,' and a spring of rue ! "

This second prologue is important, because it proves that there were reasons, apart from the imperfections

---

[1] Sheridan some years afterwards told Reynolds the playwright that during the violent opposition in the fifth act an apple hit Lee ; whereupon he stepped forward and exclaimed in rich brogue, "By the powers is it *personal.* Is it me or the matter ? " (" Reynolds's Life and Times," vol. ii. p. 227).

incidental to the rapid production of an inexperienced hand, for the temporary failure and ultimate success of "The Rivals." As an acute American critic, Mr. Brander Matthews, has recently reminded us,[1] on the authority of John Bernard, afterwards one of the first of American managers, the play was disliked by the more conservative section of the audience, who regarded it as an unwarrantable departure from the sentimental comedy then in vogue.

"Faulkland and Julia," says Bernard, "which Sheridan had obviously introduced to conciliate the sentimentalists, but which in the present day are considered incumbrances, were the characters most favourably received, whilst Sir Anthony Absolute, Bob Acres, and Lydia, those faithful and diversified pictures of life, were barely tolerated."

Sentimental comedy was moribund, but it was dying hard. Originally introduced from France, in consequence of the disfavour into which the Restoration dramatists, Wycherley, Congreve, Vanbrugh, and Farquhar, had fallen, through Jeremy Collier's formidable attack upon their inherent non-morality, this school had found its first exponent in Dick Steele, whose most successful efforts in its direction were "The Tender Husband," brought out in 1705, and "The Conscious Lovers," acted in 1722. Parson Adams, it will be remembered, found in the latter play "some things almost solemn enough for a sermon." Then followed a series of sickly plays, now deservedly forgotten: Moore's "Gamester," Whitehead's "School for Lovers," Hugh Kelly's

[1] In the preface to his critical edition of Sheridan's Comedies, published in 1885.

"False Delicacy," ending with the earlier plays of the prolific Cumberland—"The Brothers," "The East Indian," and "The Fashionable Lover." Not that sentimental comedy had the field entirely to itself. Congreve's "Love for Love" still lingered on the stage ; Wycherley's "Country Wife" had a new lease of life given it through Garrick's skilful adaptation, "The Country Girl ; " and several other Restoration plays were acted from time to time. But the occasional revivals of the Restoration drama, and the still more occasional production of a new play of merit, like " High Life below Stairs," or "The Clandestine Marriage," can have effected but little more than to keep alive the memory of what true comedy was. It is to the rough-and-ready humour of Foote that the credit of dealing the death-blow to a false school is really due. "The Sentimental Housemaid, or Piety in Pattens," contained much keen and legitimate satire upon the prevailing mode, and effected a partial reform in taste, which saved " She Stoops to Conquer " from the condemnation which would otherwise have awaited it.

A breach, then, had been made in the fortress by Foote, and Goldsmith had already carried the enemy's main position when Sheridan appeared. His was a more direct return to the Restoration drama than that attempted by Goldsmith, a writer whose sweet unreasonableness declines to come under any ordinary category. Sheridan, on the other hand, is a true disciple of Farquhar and Congreve in everything but their almost monotonous devotion to cuckoldry. The humour of " The Rivals " is racially akin to that of " The Recruiting

Sergeant" and "Beaux' Stratagem," just as the wit cf
"The School for Scandal" is of the same genus as that
of "The Way of the World" or "The Double-Dealer."
Not that Sheridan was a conscious imitator either of
Congreve or Farquhar. It is most improbable that he
sat down to make a critical examination of their writings,
and discover where they had succeeded, and where they
had failed. But a man with the dramatic instinct in him
must have felt it his duty to read such of their plays
as he had not seen on the stage, and having done so he
naturally became infected by their spirit. He saw that
there was true comedy, and in that vein he resolved to
write.

Few playwrights have been subjected to such persistent charges of plagiarism as Sheridan, and it is remarkable how insignificant really are the literary thefts that
can be proved against him. It is evident that calumny
began to wag its tongue against him as soon as "The
Rivals" was put on the stage ; and he retorted on his
assailants honestly enough, by pleading lack of learning
rather than want of invention.

"I own that, in one respect, I did not regret my ignorance ; for as
my great wish in attempting a play was to avoid every appearance
of plagiary, I thought I should stand a better chance of effecting
this from being in a walk which I had not frequented, and where,
consequently, the progress of invention was less likely to be inter-
rupted by starts of recollection ; for on subjects on which the mind
has been much informed, invention is slow of exerting itself. Faded
ideas float in the fancy like half-forgotten dreams ; and the imagination in its fullest enjoyments becomes suspicious of its offspring, and
doubts whether it has created or adopted."

Indeed, Sheridan's accusers attribute to him a knowledge of English literature, which might have been acquired after a lifetime of industrious research, but was hardly likely to be forthcoming in a young man of twenty-three, whose education had at best been desultory. Properly speaking, the only thefts that can really be brought home to him are from his mother, and thus they assume the character of possessions acquired by inheritance rather than by literary loot. As he took the name of one of his characters, Faulkland, from her novel, " Miss Sidney Biddulph," it is quite possible that he may have borrowed from the same source—-as Boaden, in his "Life of Kemble," said he had—the unimportant scene in which Faulkland puts Julia to the trial, by pretending that his life was in danger and that he was compelled to fly. Sheridan's declaration to Rogers that he had never read the novel does not go for much, for he also denied having read Wycherley, a statement very difficult of belief. More extensive were his obligations to Mrs. Sheridan's unfinished comedy, "A Trip to Bath." It has been said, indeed, that "The Rivals" was founded on the latter play. But the whole plot and most of the characters are utterly dissimilar. ' A Trip to Bath "—which, with some other manuscript plays which formerly belonged to Sheridan, was presented to the British Museum by Mr. Coventry Patmore, in 1864 —turns on the efforts of two impecunious members or society—Lady Filmot and Lord Hewkly—to secure the hands and fortunes of Edward Bull, the son of Sir Jonathan Bull, a City knight, and Lucy Tryfort, the daughter of Mrs. Tryfort, a citizen's widow. Lord Hewkly persuades Lucy to pretend to be in love with him for the purpose, as he tells her, of annoying Lady Filmot, and Lady Filmot easily induces the uncultivated Edward to act as her cicisbeo at the Assembly Rooms, arrayed as a beau in borrowed plumes. Lucy and Edward are thereupon at cross purposes, and naturally become consumed by jealousy. As an under-plot there is the courtship of Lady Bel Aircastle, a superfine lady of quality, by Champignon, a vulgar West Indian, upon whom Lord Hewkly sponges. The play breaks off at the close of the third act, when Lord Hewkly and Lady Filmot are for the time being triumphant. But as they still have a secret regard for one another, in spite of their attempts to bestow themselves elsewhere, and as Lucy's heart still beats true to Edward, it is not difficult to see how Mrs. Sheridan intended to wind up her lively comedy.

It is perfectly clear that, though the scene in both plays is laid at Bath, their plots have nothing whatever in common. Nor have the characters, with one exception, that of Mrs. Tryfort, who is undoubtedly the immediate source of Mrs. Malaprop. Several of her "derangements of epitaphs" appear in "The Rivals" with very little alteration. Mrs. Tryfort praises Lord Hewkly, "Oh, in everything, ma'am, he's a perfect progeny." Mrs. Malaprop says, "Observe me, Sir Anthony. I would by no means wish a daughter of mine to be a progeny of learning." Similarly, Mrs. Malaprop wishes that her daughter might know something of the "contagious countries;" and Mrs. Tryfort exclaims, "Oh, if you were to hear him describe contagious countries, as I have done, it would astonish you." "Sir," she says to Edward, "you are a little too pert, let me tell you, and so much taciturnity doesn't become a young man." Mrs. Malaprop, during the second scene of the second act, of "The Rivals," frequently lays down the law as to what doesn't become a young woman, "violent memories" being one of those qualities to which she takes exception. Again, Mrs. Tryfort says, "I know nothing of him [Edward], Sir Jonathan; do you think Miss Tryfort doesn't understand punctuality better than to go into corners with young men?" which may have suggested the "Female punctuation forbids me to say more" of Mrs. Malaprop's letter to Sir Lucius O'Trigger. And here are some more of Mrs. Tryfort's blunders, of which, however, Sheridan did not avail himself.

"*Mrs. Tryfort.* I declare that it is a fatiguing life one leads, and exhilitates one's spirits so much that I have scarce strength enough to rise of a morning. . . .

"*Mrs. Tryfort.* A silly chit that might be a countess if she had the grace to deserve it.

"*Lucy.* But, madam, I don't desire it.

"*Mrs. Tryfort.* There's for you, miss, a foolish metamorphosis!"

Another of the *dramatis personæ* in "A Trip to Bath" is Sir Jeremy Bull, Edward's uncle. Though as a ruined ex-member of Parliament, he has little in common with Sir Lucius O'Trigger, one of his sayings finds its way with little alteration into the Irishman's mouth. Sir Jeremy *loquitur:* "Why the land and the mansion-house have slipped thro' our fingers, boy; but, thank heaven, the family pictures are still extant." It is worth noticing, too, that one of the minor characters in "A Trip to Bath" is a lodging-house keeper, Mrs. Surface, whose house is described as "a mart of scandal," and who deals freely in that commodity while proclaiming her hatred of it. Sheridan was afterwards to borrow the name to some purpose.

Mrs. Tryfort is, then, the origin of Mrs. Malaprop, not Dogberry, or Fielding's Mrs. Slipslop, or Smollett's Mrs. Tabitha Bramble, though they are all generically akin, and though Sheridan may have borrowed from the last lady the incident of her being induced to believe that a proposal to her niece was addressed to herself. In the same way it is easy enough to find ancestors of Bob Acres, but the resemblance is never close enough to enable us to say that Sheridan deliberately copied. It is not impossible that he may have had vague recollections of Sir Andrew Ague-cheek in his mind when he wrote some of the scenes in which that hero figures. Similarly Sir Joseph Wittol, in Congreve's "Old Bachelor," anticipated Acres in the use of the "oath referential." "Gads— daggers—belts—blades—and scabbards," he exclaims, on one occasion, and his conduct, when confronted by danger, is very like that of "Fighting Bob."

"No, no," he says, "hang't I was not afraid neither—though I confess he did in a manner snap me up—yet I can't say it was altogether out of fear, but partly to prevent mischief—for he was a devilish choleric fellow : and if my choler had been up too, agad, there would have been mischief done, that's flat. . . . Adsheart, if he should come just now, when I am angry, I'd tell him—mum."

So, too, Bob's clownish efforts to learn the cotillon

remind one of the dancing-lesson of Mockmode in Farquhar's " Love and a Bottle." But the awkward and cowardly country bumpkin is surely a fairly obvious object of satire, and so is the romantic and novel-reading young lady. Sheridan certainly took a hint or two (so far as Lydia Languish was concerned) from Steele's " Tender Husband," where the niece spends her time in reading romances, is courted by her lover in disguise before her aunt's face, and agrees with Lydia that an elopement is preferable to a- common-place marriage. Again there is a Lydia Bramble in " Humphrey Clinker," of whom her uncle Matthew says, " Truly she has got a languishing eye and reads romances." The plain fact of the matter is that Mrs. Malaprop, Acres, and Lydia Languish were all more or less stock-characters, in the same way as several of the incidents in "The Rivals " had undoubtedly been used before. But the originality of the plot as a whole, and of the *dramatis personæ* as a whole, can hardly be disputed by the most determined of criticasters.

What an admirable play is " The Rivals " ! The plot is as simple as one of Farquhar's, yet there is a sufficiency of complication and an unbroken succession of humorous incidents. It is naturally and gradually developed ; for Sheridan, fortunately for himself, was not tied down to the two or three set scenes which hamper the efforts of modern playwrights, and could introduce a conversation between Sir Lucius and Lucy without being obliged to drag the pair together, in defiance of probability, into Mrs. Malaprop's drawing-room or Bob Acres' lodgings. The only instance of abruptness is the intro-

duction of the quarrel between Captain Absolute and
Sir Lucius O'Trigger. It is led up to by a single remark
in the scene in which Sir Lucius helps Acres to compose
his challenge, and we are left in the dark as to the means
by which Sir Lucius became aware that Captain Absolute,
qua Absolute, was a suitor for the hand of Lydia Languish.
Possibly some elucidatory matter went by the board after
the two disastrous performances of the play, and we can
be well content to rest satisfied with Sir Lucius' remark,
" The quarrel is a very pretty quarrel as it stands ; we
should only spoil it by trying to explain it." The blemish is
indeed microscopic, and carries little weight in the critical
balance when opposed to the ingenuity of the truly
delightful scene (act iii. scene 3) between Mrs. Malaprop,
Captain Absolute, and Lydia Languish. Therein the
captain is twice on the brink of exposure, and is saved
on the first occasion by his own ready tongue, on the
second by Lydia's unwitting use of ambiguous phrases,
which are yet so easily introduced that the dialogue does
not strike you as being in any degree forced.

It has been said, with some truth, that the loves of
Faulkland and Julia have little to do with the main
development of the plot. But two pairs of lovers were
the regulation number, and until they get together Faulkland and Julia are both quite tolerable. Indeed, in the
scenes with Captain Absolute the morbid and suspicious
character of Faulkland makes an excellent foil to the
easy-going and cocksure disposition of the captain.
Nothing can be better in its way than Faulkland's outcry
on hearing that Julia had been engaged in his absence in
country dances:—

" Now disappointment on her ! Defend this, Absolute ; why don't you defend this ? Country dances ! jigs and reels ! Am I to blame now ? A minuet I could have forgiven ; I should not have minded that—I say I should not have regarded a minuet—but country dances ! Zounds ! had she made one in a cotillon I believe I should have forgiven even that ! But to be monkey-led for a night !—to run the gauntlet through a string of amorous palming puppies ! to show paces like a managed filly ! Oh, Jack ! there never can be but one man in the world whom a truly modest and delicate woman ought to pair with in a country dance ; and, even then, the rest of the couples should be her great-uncles and aunts ! "

When Faulkland and Julia are alone together it must be acknowledged that they are tiresome. But for years after the production of the play they were taken quite seriously, and Professor Smyth, in his little memoir of Sheridan, tells us that the audience used to melt into tears as it listened to them. Now people yawn. Sheridan, however, was wise in his generation, when he wrote the scenes in which they figure, and introduced into them some of his most elaborate ornamentation. His object was immediate success rather than the applause of posterity, which is of singularly little assistance towards the filling of an empty purse. He therefore made a concession to the prevailing taste, and made it in sober earnestness. It would be an anachronism, though a tempting one, no doubt, to imagine that he wrote with his tongue in his cheek when he penned their high-flown sentimentalities. Though he cut himself free from genteel comedy, he could hardly fail to be influenced by it to a certain degree, and probably a good deal more than he was at all aware.

Good in its way though the plot of " The Rivals " is,

the merits of the play depend upon its characters and its dialogue. Both of these are true rather to the stage than to nature, and "The Rivals," like all Sheridan's plays, gains immensely by representation. It has indeed been suggested that Sheridan in this play transcribed his own experiences of life. According to that theory Captain Absolute's pursuit of Lydia Languish was suggested by his own courtship of Miss Linley, and the duel scene by his own combats with Mathews. But the facts in the two cases are utterly dissimilar—in the one there was not, in the other there was, an elopement; in the one there was not, in the other there was, a duel. And though Mrs. Sheridan's character, as portrayed by Professor Smyth on the somewhat malevolent authority of her neighbour, Mrs. Canning, does bear a faint resemblance to that of Lydia Languish, the identification is the merest guesswork. In fact, the only supposition that has any real probability is that which identifies Sheridan himself with Faulkland, and here again there are difficulties in the way of proof. The keynote to the differences of Faulkland and Julia is that they have been destined for each other by her father. She says, " I see you are determined to be unkind! The contract which my poor father bound us in gives you more than a lover's privilege." And he replies, " Again, Julia, you raise ideas that feed and justify my doubts. I would not have been more free —no—I am proud of my restraint. Yet—yet—perhaps your high respect alone for this solemn compact has fettered your inclinations, which else had made a worthier choice." Now old Sheridan's opposition to his son's marriage was most determined. Besides, as Mr. Brander

Matthews has pointed out, Sheridan, who would not let his wife sing in public, was the last man in the world to put the story of his courtship on the stage. The jealous lover is a common enough figure in comedy in all conscience, and if we must have a prototype for Faulkland, a fairly evident one can be found in the Valentine of Wycherley's "Love in a Wood."

The more strongly drawn characters of the play are still more obviously the creations of Sheridan's brain, aided by hints from novels that he had read and plays that he had seen. Sheridan, when he wrote "The Rivals," though his experience of life had been varied and considerable, was too young to have made a deep study of human nature. Even with ripened knowledge he never attempted to go beneath the surface of character, but remained to the last content to reproduce external oddities, and the current manners of society. He could create an Acres, but could not create a Falstaff. He certainly never attempted to do so, and no one in their senses ever dreamt of comparing him with Shakespeare or Molière; he is altogether on a different and lower plane. Nor did he ever desire to make his characters conform to, or depart from, other than a purely conventional system of morality, and even within those limits troubled himself little with consistency compared with effect. He knew his limits; he knew perfectly well that he could never have written "The Alchemist" or "Volpone," with their solemn purpose and deep philosophy of life. Accordingly he remained to the last as purely non-moral as Congreve or Vanbrugh; and, though he indirectly did lip-service to the Young

Person by refraining from making cuckoldry the sole pivot of his plays, it may be suspected that in his heart of hearts he cordially despised her, and wished that she was abolished.

Even in the artificial world to which he confined himself, the world of the footlights, Sheridan in this his first play not unfrequently outrages probability ; Bob Acres and Mrs. Malaprop are deliberate caricatures. The lady's verbal misapplications, especially, are too elaborate and too constant for art. Sheridan had got hold of a good idea, and he rode it to death. An uneducated woman who attempts fine language is liable to ludicrous mistakes enough, but she would never have uttered the volleys of absurdities which occur in Mrs. Malaprop's celebrated discourse on education. Her more ornate flights of blundering—" Sure if I reprehend anything in the world it is the use of my oracular tongue and a nice derangement of epitaphs," for instance—are so elaborately ingenious that they are evidently not the natural utterances of the character, but the conscious efforts of the dramatist. So, too, Acres' absurdities are too numerous and too unrelieved by any redeeming quality. He is a combination of a poltroon and a would-be man of fashion, with the attributes of both exaggerated, and his oaths fit the occasion far too well to have been elaborated by the intelligence of a country squire. In fact, he treads dangerously near the well-defined border-line which separates comedy from farce. But again we can only say that Sheridan's comedy is intended for the theatre not the study, and for the edification of the pit as well as that of the stalls. When we see it upon the stage our criticism is fairly disarmed by laughter, and it is only reasonable to judge a playwright by canons which he would have himself acknowledged. Acres may be more than forgiven for the duel scene.

Far more subtle than Mrs. Malaprop and Acres are the characters of Sir Lucius O'Trigger and Sir Anthony Absolute. Why the audience took offence at the former must pass the wit of man to decide. He is thoroughly well-bred; even the flippant Lucy acknowledges that he has "too much pride and delicacy to sacrifice the feelings of a gentleman to the necessities of his fortune;" and when his schemes have failed he treats Mrs. Malaprop with a degree of consideration which she but ill requites by calling him a Vandyke. It is evident that Sheridan at first intended to put a string of bulls into his mouth. Sir Lucius begins well by informing Lucy that the probable reason why they did not meet was because he was on the South Parade and she was on the North, and that "it is very comical too how you should go out and I not see you, for I was only taking a nap at the Parade Coffee House." But Sheridan probably came to the conclusion that bulls in addition to Mrs. Malaprop's blunders would be rather too large an order, and Sir Lucius was confined to the grim humours of, "I'm told there's very snug lying in the Abbey." Sir Anthony is an altogether delightful personage, superior by an immense altitude to the ordinary choleric father of comedy. Excellent is the touch, "Damn me if ever I call you Jack again," and still better his delight when he imagines that Captain Absolute has been too free with Lydia Languish. "Come, no excuses, Jack; why, your father, you rogue, was so before you—the blood of the Absolutes was always impatient." The scene (act iii. scene 1) in which he describes the charms of Lydia Languish, and is suddenly thrown into a fury by the question, " Which is to be mine, sir, the niece or the aunt ? " is, as Moore points out, perhaps the best in the comedy. But it is unnecessary to quote a passage from a play which is easily accessible, and in which many of the present generation have probably had the privilege of seeing Mr. William Farren.

The dialogue of " The Rivals " is not so exquisitely polished as that of " The School for Scandal," and, if less effective on the stage, it is a good deal more natural. Probably the very haste in which the play was written saved it from over-elaboration, not that there is the slightest trace of slovenliness from first to last. On the contrary, the balance of sentence is maintained throughout, and how a young man, whose education had been limited, and who could not spell, contrived to turn out such excellent prose is a question that can be more easily asked than answered. No doubt, however, the lessons in rhetoric which he had received from his father were of considerable benefit to him, for much of the dialogue, notably Faulkland's longer speeches and Captain Absolute's outburst to Lydia Languish in scene 3 of act iii., looks as if it had been formed on oratorical models. But discussions on the origin of style are apt to be conjectural rather than improving. It would be fatuous to deny there are to be found in the play numerous instances of that false ornamentation from which nothing either written or spoken by Sheridan was ever entirely

free. The tag with which Julia brings down the curtain
in the last act is a glaring instance, and Sir Anthony
Absolute's description of the circulating library is far too
elaborate to be put in the mouth even of a stage country
gentleman.

"*Sir Anth.* Madam, a circulating library in a town is as an
evergreen tree of diabolical knowledge ! It blossoms through the
year !—and, depend upon it, Mrs. Malaprop, that they who are
so fond of handling the leaves will long for the fruit at last."

The inappropriateness of the dialogue to the character to whom it is assigned is of course more conspicuous
when we come to the servants. Thomas is indeed an
exception. Thomas says little that might not be forthcoming from a rustic humourist, and, what is more, talks
very fair Devonshire—" a mort " for a heap or a quan-
tity, and " the stuff " for money, being still common
expressions in that county. But David's remark that
our ancestors are very good kind of folks, but they are
the last people he would choose to have a visiting
acquaintance with, seems rather out of place, and Fag's
conceits especially smack of the drawing-room not of
the servants' hall, notably the famous classical allusion
to "Love who has been a masquerader ever since the
days of Jupiter." But if Sheridan sinned in making his
valets as witty and cultured as their masters, he sinned
in very good company. Congreve's servants all talk the
language of good society, and more than one man-ser-
vant of the Restoration drama airs his knowledge of
Latin and Greek. Thus Jeremy in "Love for Love,"
who to be sure had been a gyp at Cambridge, is learned

about Nilus, and Scrub in "The Beaux' Stratagem"
exclaims on very slight provocation, "Cedunt arma togæ."
It may well be that a young man of twenty-three was too
impressed with the merits of his masters to note their
defects. But Sheridan was always wide awake, and it is
more probable that he had a shrewd inkling that by
making—to use Macaulay's phrase—his characters in
his own likeness, his play would command the applause
of the playgoer, though it might earn the censure of the
psychologist. And, after all, the exhibition of too much
wit is a fault on the right side.

CHAPTER III.

"THE RIVALS" ran at Covent Garden for fourteen nights, and was a most unqualified success in the provinces, notably at Bath, Bristol, and Southampton. But Sheridan was not at all inclined to rest on his laurels. Out of gratitude to Clinch, who had so largely helped to save "The Rivals," he wrote for that actor's benefit the farce called "St. Patrick's Day, or, The Scheming Lieutenant." It was brought out on the 2nd of May, 1775, and was acted six times before the close of the season.

"St. Patrick's Day" no longer holds the stage, and its six changes of scene in two short acts are no doubt a serious consideration against its revival in the present days of solid and costly accessories. But it is a bright little farce, obviously founded, much as was Wycherley's "Gentleman Dancing-master," upon Molière. Of Molière in the original Sheridan probably knew little, for his acquaintance with the French language was very limited, and when he and Dundas thought fit to discuss the meaning of the word "malheureux"—pronounced "maleroo"—in a despatch, the House of Commons laughed at them consumedly. But it is obvious that he must have studied the great French dramatist, notably his "École des Femmes," in some translation, when he rattled off "St. Patrick's Day."

The story is simple enough, but is perhaps worth re-telling. Lieutenant O'Connor is in love with Lauretta, the daughter of Justice Credulous, but the old man will not hear of the match. Accordingly the Lieutenant persuades his friend Dr. Rosy to present him to the Justice in the disguise of a countryman, Humphrey Hum, who is recommended as Lauretta's guardian against the desperate schemes of O'Connor. At first all goes well; the disguised Lieutenant administers a mock beating to three of his own soldiers, and wins the entire confidence of Credulous. But he is promptly discovered kissing the young lady, and ordered off the premises. His discomfiture is short, however, as he quickly sends a letter to Credulous, in which he declares that he has that morning administered a dose of poison to the Justice in his chocolate. In great alarm, Credulous accepts Rosy's suggestion that a German quack, who is hard by, should be called in to administer an antidote. The quack is O'Connor in a fresh disguise; he declares himself prepared to restore the Justice if he will consent to his union with Lauretta, and then writes the prescription, "In reading this you are cured, by your affectionate son-in-law, O'Connor." Credulous is naturally furious, but comes to the conclusion he will at any rate disappoint his wife's obvious anxiety to get hold of his estate, and surrenders the girl to her lover. The dialogue is suffi-ciently amusing, though not in Sheridan's best manner. Dr. Rosy's moralizings to his departed Dolly are capital

—"such an arm for a bandage—veins that seemed to
invite the lancet.   Then her skin, smooth and white as
a gallipot."   So too is Mrs. Credulous's description of a
soldier husband.

" Oh, barbarous ! to want a husband that may wed you to-day,
and be sent the Lord knows where before night ; then in a
twelvemonth perhaps to have him come like a Colossus, with one
leg at New York and the other at Chelsea Hospital."

All through the summer Sheridan worked hard at a
comic opera, the music of which was selected and composed by his father-in-law, Mr. Linley.   The pair conducted their labours chiefly by correspondence, as Linley
had a professional engagement at Bath, and Sheridan's
letters, as published by Moore, are interesting as showing
the unmethodical energy which he could, when he chose,
put into his work.   He was most minute and persistent
in his hints to Mr. Linley, and though he had no tech-
nical training in music, yet he displayed much practical
knowledge of its effect upon the stage.   No doubt he
was helped to a very considerable extent by his accomplished wife.   " Dearest father," she writes, " I have no
spirits or hopes of the opera unless we see you," and it
will be observed that Sheridan, in his directions to Mr.
Linley, speaks in the plural more often than in the
singular.

" The enclosed are the words for 'Wind, gentle evergreen ; ' a
passionate song for Mattocks, and another for Miss Brown, which I
solicit to be clothed in melody by you, and are all I want.   Mattocks's I could wish to be a broken, passionate affair, and the first
two lines may be recitative, or what you please, uncommon.   Miss

Brown sings hers in a joyful mood : we want her to show in it as much execution as she is capable of, which is pretty well ; and, for variety, we want Mr. Simpson's hautboy to cut a figure with replying passages, &c., in the way of Fisher's ' *M'ami il bel idol mio,*' to abet which I have lugged in Echo, who is always allowed to play her part."[1]

Mr. Linley, though he submitted in the end, seems at first to have resented the dictation of a young spark, who did not know a note of music, while his artistic feelings were outraged by the use that was made of other people's compositions, though he might have found consolation in the example of " The Beggar's Opera." He vented his feelings in a letter to Garrick, which is to be found in the Garrick Correspondence.

" I have promised to assist Sheridan in compiling—I believe this is the properest term—an opera, which I understand from him he has engaged to produce at Covent Garden this season. I have already set some airs which he has given me, and he intends writing new words to some tunes of mine. My son has likewise written some tunes for him, and I understand he is to have some others from Mr. Jackson of Exeter. This is a mode of proceeding in regard to his composition which I by no means approve of. I think he ought first to have finished his opera with the songs he intends to introduce into it, and have got it entirely new set. No musician

---

[1] Mattocks' song was finally omitted. He was the Don Ferdinand of the piece. But Miss Brown's is Donna Clara's song in the third act.

> " Adieu, thou dreary pile, where never dies
> The sullen echo of repentant sighs !
> Ye sister mourners of each lonely cell
> Inured to hymns and sorrow, fare ye well !
> For happier scenes I fly this lonesome grove
> To saints a prison, but a tomb to love.'"

can set a song properly unless he understands the character and knows the performer who is to exhibit it. . . . I would not have been concerned in this business at all, but that I know there is an absolute necessity for him to endeavour to get some money by th's means, and he will not be persuaded upon to let his wife sing, and indeed at present she is incapable, and nature will not permit me to be indifferent to his success."

Every one with whom Sheridan had to work was inclined from time to time to kick against his disorderly method of procedure, but in the end they had little cause to regret the partnership. Mr. Linley would have written in a very different strain after the piece was fairly launched.

"The Duenna" was performed at Covent Garden on the 21st of November, 1775. It had an unprecedented run of seventy-five nights, as against the sixty-three of "The Beggar's Opera." Moore declares that its attractions seriously diminished the audiences at Drury Lane. Garrick, he tells us, was even compelled to have recourse to the expedient of playing off the mother against the son by reviving Mrs. Sheridan's comedy, "The Discovery." "The old woman," it was said, "would be the death of the old man." But the story is obviously absurd. There is contemporary evidence that Drury Lane was drawing enormous houses, Garrick's approaching retirement from the stage having already been hinted abroad. Besides, the English Roscius was at this time in treaty with Sheridan for the purchase of his share of the theatre, and the revival of his mother's comedy, if made with any deliberate intention, was far more likely to have been made in the spirit of compliment than of rivalry. It seems Garrick only acted Sir

Anthony Branville six nights, and the simple explanation would appear to be that, as one of his favourite and less fatiguing parts, it was assumed without any afterthought whatever.

Much of the popularity of " The Duenna " was evidently gained by the music, of which what was not Mr. Linley's was selected from the well-known airs of Dr. Harrington, Rauzzini, Jackson, and other composers. But Sheridan's songs have intrinsic merits, and are deservedly remembered apart from their setting. Though, perhaps, of no very high order of poetry—Sheridan was never more than a writer of clever verses—they are far superior in literary execution to the halting rhymes and florid sentiments of ordinary comic opera, and are at once sparkling and refined. Curiously enough Sheridan's livelier efforts are hardly so successful as those in which he appealed to the gentler emotions of his audience. Don Jerome's, " Oh, the days when I was young," once in the mouth of every street-boy, is now almost forgotten. But " Had I a heart for falsehood framed," " I ne'er could any lustre see," and " Oh, had my love ne'er smiled on me," seem secure of immortality, though " The Duenna " left the stage with Braham. Perhaps the most ambitious song in the opera is Donna Clara's, in the fifth scene of the first act, and it comes nearest to true poetry, in spite of Moore's rather captious objection to the fourth line :

> " When sable night, each drooping plant restoring,
> Wept o'er the flowers her breath did cheer,
> As some sad widow o'er her babe deploring,
> Wakes its beauty with a tear :

4

When all did sleep, whose weary hearts did borrow
One hour from love and care to rest ;
Lo ! as I press'd my couch in silent sorrow,
My lover caught me to his breast ! "

The plot of "The Duenna" contains some ingenious
though rather common-place complications, and is quite
sufficient for its three acts, without placing a very severe
strain upon the intellectual faculties of the audience.
Moore thinks that the central incident was suggested by
the scene in Wycherley's " Country Girl," in which Mrs.
Pinchwife escapes from the house of her jealous husband
in her sister-in-law's clothes.   But disguise is surely common enough in comic opera, and the general scheme of
" The Duenna " seems to suggest Molière rather than
Wycherley.   As the opera is never acted now, and but
little read, a short description of the plot may not be
amiss.   It turns upon the efforts of Don Jerome to prevent his daughter Louisa from marrying her lover, Don
Antonio, by forcing her into matrimony with Isaac, a
recently converted Jew.   The girl and the Duenna
together contrive to outwit the old man.   The Duenna
is caught by him in the act of conveying a letter from
Antonio, and is promptly ordered out of the house.   It
is however Louisa, disguised in the old woman's cardinal
and veil, not the Duenna, who is turned out.   She meets
her friend Donna Clara, an old flame of Antonio's, but
now in love with Louisa's brother Ferdinand, though
there is a temporary coolness between the pair owing
to his importunity.   Clara is about to take refuge in a
convent from her lover and stepmother, and thither
Louisa resolves to follow her if she can find Antonio.

This she effects through Isaac himself, who has never seen her, and is therefore easily gulled by her use of Clara's name into bringing the lovers together in his own lodgings. The second act opens with Isaac's courtship of the Duenna, who has been locked by Don Jerome into her mistress's room, and the scenes in which his expectations are excited by the old man's enthusiastic descriptions of his daughter's charms, only to be dashed to the ground by the sight of the hideous old harridan, are extremely amusing, though the humour is occasionally not far removed from vulgarity. It is needless to state that the Jew's cupidity gets the better of his disappointment, and he readily accepts the Duenna's proposal that he should elope with her. After some incidental scenes the two pairs of lovers meet at a Priory; there Clara and Ferdinand are reconciled, and they all—including Isaac and the Duenna, who have also found their way thither—are united in wedlock by a jovial monk, Father Paul. The usual explanations follow at Don Jerome's house, and with the forgiveness of the lovers and the discomfiture of Isaac, the curtain falls.

The characters in "The Duenna" are conventional, and there is little attempt to give them individuality with the exception of Isaac. He is very well drawn, supremely proud of his own cleverness, "roguish, you'll say, but keen, hey? devilish keen!" and invariably made the dupe of every one whom he comes across. Originally he was supplied with a friend of the same stamp, styled Cousin Moses; but the part was cut down—either, as Moore says, because it would apply too personally to its creator Leoni, or, according to another story, because

Leoni's English was limited—until there remains an unimportant and colourless person called Carlos. The
Duenna herself has few distinguishing features beyond
her ugliness, which is made the subject of some very
homespun wit on the part of Isaac; and the airy Antonio,
the jealous Ferdinand, and the irascible Don Jerome are
little better than the ghosts of Captain Absolute, Faulkland, and Sir Anthony. Sheridan probably thought that
elaboration of character and pointed dialogue were
wasted on a comic opera, and it is quite possible that
more than one member of the company may have been,
as Sir Walter Scott said of Braham, Leoni's successor
in the part of Carlos, "a beast of an actor, though an
angel of a singer." He certainly troubled himself
remarkably little about local colour, any more than did
Vanbrugh in his least satisfactory comedy, "The False
Friend," the scene of which is also laid in Spain. It was
enough that the dialogue was bright and easily delivered ;
he seems to have aimed at little more. Here and there
is a touch of his own peculiar fancy ; for instance, the
description of the recently converted Jew, Isaac, "standing like a blank page between the Old and the New
Testament." But, on the whole, "The Duenna" does
not contain much that is really worthy of him, and
Byron was but a partial critic when, by styling it "the
best opera" in our language, he ranked it above Gay's
masterpiece with its Captain Macheath and Polly
Peachum.

Certain it is that Sheridan does not seem to have
set great store by the book of the opera. He never
took the trouble to revise any of the printed editions,

and several of them do not include one of its best
songs, " Ah, cruel maid, .how hast thou chang'd."
Many years afterwards, in 1807, Kelly the musician
and singer, left the printed play of " The Duenna "
on his table, after looking over the part of Ferdinand which he was to perform that evening. On his
return home he found Sheridan reading it, and cor-
recting it as he read. To his question, " Do you act the
part of Ferdinand from this printed copy ? " Kelly replied
in the affirmative, and added that he had done so for
twenty years. " Then," said Sheridan, " you have been
acting great nonsense," and corrected every sentence
before he left the room. The corrections were preserved
by Kelly in Sheridan's own handwriting, but he does not
seem to have published them. It is quite possible, then,
that the text of " The Duenna " is not particularly correct. But, at least, it does not seem to be disfigured by
the gags of subsequent generations of actors, though a
very vulgar interpolation is constantly introduced on the
present stage into Bob Acres' challenge in "The Rivals,"
though a meaningless " I'll take my oath of that " is put
into the mouth of Moses in " The School for Scandal,"
and though " The Critic " is translated out of all recog-
nition by extravagant business and exaggerated clowning.

CHAPTER IV.

A FIVE-ACT comedy, a two-act farce, and a three-act comic opera, were not a bad year's work. At the beginning of 1775 Sheridan was an unknown literary tyro; at its close the first dramatist of his time. He was in great request as a writer of prologues and epilogues, a class of composition peculiarly suited to his somewhat ostentatious muse. Thus to Savage's tragedy of "Sir Thomas Overbury," which was revived at Covent Garden in February, 1777, he contributed a prologue which contained a well-turned compliment to Savage's biographer, Dr. Johnson :—

> " So pleads the tale that gives to future times
> The son's misfortunes, and the parents' crimes.
> There shall his fame (if own'd to-night) survive,
> Fixed by the hand that bids our language live."

The Doctor was evidently delighted by the young man's discriminating praise, and hastened to return the compliment. Some six weeks afterwards he proposed, and of course carried, the election of Sheridan as a member of the Literary Club, observing : "He who has written the two best comedies of the age is surely a considerable man." [1]

Meanwhile Sheridan, in conjunction with Linley and Dr. Ford, was in communication with Garrick for the purchase of his share in Drury Lane Theatre, and the bargain, after many delays, was concluded in June, 1776. The theatre was valued at £70,000, so that Garrick's half was worth £35,000. It was agreed that Dr. Ford should find £15,000; Sheridan and Mr. Linley £10,000 each. Whence Sheridan obtained the money has, until recent years, been a mystery, for not only did he raise the original £10,000, but two years later, dissensions having arisen between the new partners and Willoughby Lacy, the last was bought out by Sheridan for "a price exceeding £45,000." But Mr. Brander Matthews can fairly claim to have solved the difficulty. Here is his most ingenious explanation :—

"Of the original £35,000 paid Garrick, Sheridan was to find £10,000. Dr. Watkins asserts that he raised £8,700 of this £10,000 by two mortgages, one of £1,000 to a Mr. Wallis, and another of £7,700 to Dr. Ford. If we accept this assertion—and I see no reason why we should not—all that Sheridan had to make up was £1,300, a sum which he could easily compass after the success of 'The Rivals' and 'The Duenna,' even supposing he did not encroach on, or had already exhausted, the £3,000 settled on his wife by Mr. Long. . . . A note in Sheridan's handwriting, quoted by Moore, states that Lacy was paid 'a price exceeding £45,000,' which would go to show that the total value of the property had risen in two years from £70,000 to £90,000. Most writers on the subject have taken this note of Sheridan's to mean

---

[1] That is, " The Rivals " and " The Duenna," though the latter is hardly a comedy.

that he paid at least £45,000 in cash, and they have all exhausted
their efforts in guessing where he got the money. But if we compare
Moore's statement with Watkins's we get nearer a solution of the
difficulty. Watkins says that Lacy's share was already mortgaged
for £31,500, and that Sheridan assumed the mortgage, and agreed
further to pay in return for the equity of redemption two annuities
at £500 each. This double obligation (the mortgage for £31,500
and the annuities) represents 'a price exceeding £45,000,' but did
not require a single penny in cash. On the contrary, the purchase
of Lacy's half of the theatre actually put money into Sheridan's
pocket, for he at once divided his original one-seventh between
Linley and Dr. Ford, making each of their shares up to one-fourth;
and even if they paid him no increase on the original price, he would
have been enabled to pay off the £8,700 mortgages to Dr. Ford
and to Mr. Wallis, and to get back the £1,300 which he seems to
have advanced himself. In fact, it appears that Sheridan invested
only £1,300 in cash when he bought one-seventh of Drury Lane
Theatre in 1776, and that he received this back when he became
possessed of one-half of Drury Lane Theatre in 1778, then valued
at £90,000." [1]

[1] Among the documents quoted in *The English Illustrated Magazine* is a memorandum of Sheridan's anent the purchase of Lacy's
share, in which the figures differ from those of Dr. Watkins and
Moore, but not to such an extent as to affect materially Mr. Brander
Matthews's argument. Supposing it to be genuine—and it certainly
looks so—we may have in it the final terms of an agreement, of
which Moore could only discover the preliminary negotiations.
The figures are :—

Exceeding £31,000	
The *share* in the debt of the new management, *much* to be attributed to Mr. Lacy	1,500
To pay him in money, every shilling paid ...	7,500
To secure on the theatre an annuity of £1,000 on the lives of Langford and Mr. Lacy £500 each	16,000
	£56,000

Dr. Watkins further suggests that when Sheridan borrowed the £7,700 from Dr. Ford, Garrick stood behind Ford. But the last statement is certainly incorrect. It appears from the Garrick Papers (vol. ii. p. 293) that Garrick had already lent £22,000 to Lacy on mortgage, which he allowed to remain on loan under the new partnership. The careful David certainly did not lend any more, for when, shortly afterwards, he found it necessary to press the new management for his interest, the £22,000 alone is mentioned, and nothing is said about a new loan (Ibid. p. 303). So that the legend about Garrick having come to the rescue of a brother genius in distress must be abandoned. His assistance was purely negative, and consisted in his not withdrawing his money from the speculation, and that after all was something. But Drury Lane was evidently regarded as good security, for Linley had no difficulty in raising his money at four per cent. Whether, therefore, Dr. Ford was financially sound, or whether he was a man of straw with a " Little Premium " at his back, does not seem to be a very important question.

The new management opened on September 21, 1776, and did not begin well. Sheridan had nothing ready, and was compelled to fall back upon " The Rivals," transferred from Covent Garden, and a revival of Congreve's " Old Bachelor." Nor did " Semiramis," an indifferent tragedy by Captain Ayscough, remedy matters, though Sheridan contributed an epilogue to it, in which the lady spectator was bade—

> " Go, search, where keener woes demand relief,
> Go, while thy heart yet beats with fancied grief ;

Thy lip still conscious of the recent sigh,
The grateful tear still quivering in thine eye.
Go—and on real misery bestow
The blest effusions of fictitious woe."

Worse was to follow. In October Lacy attempted to
infringe the deed of partnership by introducing two
new partners into the business. Sheridan thereupon
took the extreme step of seceding from the theatre for
several days, and the actors, following his example,
shammed sickness when summoned by the prompter.
King and Smith, the future Sir Peter Teazle and Charles
Surface, were chief among the malingerers. To Sheridan
the whole affair seemed an excellent joke, and he wrote
to Garrick on the 15th :—

"Indeed, never was known such an uncommon epidemic disorder
as has raged among our unfortunate company ; it differs only from
the plague by attacking the better sort first. The manner, too, in
which they are seized, I am told, is very extraordinary ; many who
were in perfect health at one moment, on receiving a billet from
the prompter to summon them to business, are seized with sudden
qualms, and before they can get through the contents, are absolutely
unfit to leave their rooms ; so that Hopkins's notes seem to operate
like what we hear of Italian poisoned letters, which strike with sickness those to whom they are addressed. In short, if a successful
author had given the company a dinner at Salt Hill, the effects
could not be more injurious to our dramatic representatives."

His imperturbability carried the day. Lacy was compelled to write an apology to the public, and Sheridan
returned to his duties. But it is evident that harmony
did not long continue, for two years later Lacy, as we
have seen, was bought out.

During all these troubles Garrick continued to advise Sheridan, and it was probably on his instigation that the new manager wrote, as his first contribution to the stock of Drury Lane, an adaptation of Vanbrugh's comedy, "The Relapse," which was brought out on the 24th of February, 1777, under the title of "A Trip to Scarborough." At first the audience would not have it on any terms; they wanted Sheridan, not Bowdlerized Vanbrugh. Lord Foppington—stap his vitals—failed to please, though played by Dodd, the creator of Sir Benjamin Backbite; and even the conjunction on the stage of the wit of Mrs. Abington and the beauty of Miss Farren and Mrs. Robinson was not acceptable. But before many years had passed "A Trip to Scarborough" had become a favourite play, and Mrs. Jordan's Miss Hoyden was always considered one of that charming actress's most popular impersonations. Even at the present day "A Trip to Scarborough," if well acted, would be sure of a good run. For Sheridan has succeeded in a task before which the most courageous of modern adapters would probably quail. He has contrived, to quote Garrick's prologue—

> "To draw some slender covering o'er
> That graceless wit which was too bare before "—

without material injury to Lord Foppington, perhaps the best individual character in the whole range of the Restoration drama.[1]

[1] The allusion is to Pope's line—

> "And Van wants grace that never wanted wit.'

Since the above paragraph was written a successful adaptation

It is possible that "A Trip to Scarborough" was only intended by Sheridan for a stop-gap, for he was hard at work on "The School for Scandal," which was at length performed on the 8th of May, 1777. The anxiety of those concerned in its production must have been considerable. Though Garrick was keenly interested in the comedy, to which he contributed the prologue, Sheridan was behindhand with the dialogue, as was afterwards the case with "The Critic" and "Pizarro." The play was announced before the copy was in the hands of the actors, and the last five scenes had to be dashed off *currente calamo*. "Finished at last, thank God," wrote Sheridan on the last leaf, to which outburst of piety Hopkins the prompter added a cordial "Amen." But another trial was in store for the management. On the night before the performance the license was refused, on the ground that Moses was regarded as a satire on a money-lender who had recently been before the public as a candidate for the office of city chamberlain in opposition to Wilkes. Sheridan easily persuaded Lord Hertford, the Lord Chamberlain, to grant the license; but for the moment he must have thought that the stars were fighting against him. When the play was at last produced and had gained an unequivocal triumph, it was only natural that, as he told Lord Byron, he should have got very drunk, and have been taken to the watch-house for making a row in the street.

"The School for Scandal" ran twenty nights in its

of "The Relapse," by Mr. Robert Buchanan, has been produced at the Vaudeville Theatre, under the title of "Miss Tom-boy."

first season, and sixty-five in its second. For several years
it continued to be acted regularly three nights a week,
and brought in nearly twice as much as any other play.
" 'The School for Scandal,' " recorded the Treasurer
of Drury Lane in 1779, "damped the new pieces."
It has retained its extraordinary popularity throughout the present century. It has been revived times
without number in England and the United States,
and has been translated into nearly every European
language and even into Hindustani. But though nearly
every great actor since Sheridan's time has been asso-
ciated with "The School for Scandal," it may fearlessly
be asserted that no collective performance, and few
individual impersonations, have ever equalled those of
the company which created the play. Horace Walpole
records that there were "more parts performed admirably
in 'The School for Scandal' than he almost ever saw in
any play." Charles Lamb too declares that "no piece
was ever so completely cast in all its parts as this
manager's comedy," and Lamb saw the whole of the
original company except Smith who had been succeeded
in Charles Surface by Kemble, and Mrs. Abington who
had been followed as Lady Teazle by Miss Farren.
Indeed it is evident that Sheridan, as every good dramatist should, deliberately set himself to fit a company,
which, unlike that of "The Rivals," consisted of actors
who were already at the top of their profession. He
told Rogers that he did not bring Charles Surface and
Maria together until the last act, because neither Smith
nor Miss Hopkins could safely be trusted with a love
scene. Otherwise Smith, the Delaunay of his time, must

have been an ideal Charles; and his successor Kemble,
rather to our astonishment, is described by Lamb as
having been very good. " His harshest tones became
steeped and dulcified in good humour. He made his
defects a grace. Not one of his sparkling sentences
was lost." But the performer whom Lamb selects for
special praise is John Palmer, who by his consummate
acting made Joseph Surface rather than Charles the hero
of the piece, with his "gay boldness, the graceful solemn
plausibility, the measured step, the insinuating voice—to
express it in a word—the downright *acted* villainy of the
part." King, too, the original Lord Ogleby of "The
Clandestine Marriage," was admirable as Sir Peter
Teazle ; so were Parsons as Crabtree and Dodd as Sir
Benjamin Backbite ; Baddeley as Moses gave one of his
elaborate studies of Jewish character. Miss Pope, the
Mrs. Candour, was, says Lamb, "the perfect gentlewoman
as distinguished from the fine lady of comedy." Mrs.
Abington was forty when she first played Lady Teazle,
but no one seems to have thought that she looked too old
for the part. On the contrary, Horace Walpole describes
her acting in the character as equal to the first of her
profession, as superior to any effort of Garrick's ; she
seemed to him, indeed, "the very person." About her
successor, Miss Farren, Charles Lamb is rather un-
gallantly silent, but Sheridan thought highly of her.
"God bless you," he said when she retired from the
stage, " Lady Teazle is no more, and 'The School for
Scandal' has broke up for the holidays." Altogether one
can well understand the force of Lamb's contention that
' amid the mortifying circumstances attendant upon grow-

ing old, it was something to have seen 'The School for Scandal' in its glory."

"The School for Scandal" depended a good deal on its interpretation, for it is like "The Rivals" distinctly a play to be heard sooner than read. Its wit is brilliant rather than subtle, and its characters lend themselves to exhibition rather than study. Hazlitt, in his "Lectures on the Comic Writers," has well described the spectacular nature of Sheridan's talents, which find their best expression in his masterpiece, "The School for Scandal."

"This," he says, "is the merit of Sheridan's comedies, that everything in them *tells*; there is no labour in vain. His comic muse does not go about prying into obscure corners, or collecting idle curiosities, but shows her laughing face, and points to her rich treasure—the follies of mankind. She is garlanded and crowned with roses and vine-leaves. Her eyes sparkle with delight, and her heart runs over with good-natured malice. Her step is firm and light, and her ornaments consummate! 'The School for Scandal' is, if not the most original, perhaps the most finished and faultless comedy which we have. When it is acted you hear people round you exclaiming, ' Surely it is impossible for anything to be cleverer.' The scene in which Charles sells all the old family pictures but his uncle's, who is the purchaser in disguise, and that of the discovery of Lady Teazle when the screen falls, are among the happiest and most highly wrought that comedy in its wide and brilliant range can boast."

The opinion of Horace Walpole upon matters of taste is always entitled to respect even where it fails to command acquiescence, and though considerably less favourable, it was much the same as Hazlitt's. "There is," he wrote, "a deal of wit and good situations; but it is too long, has two or three bad scenes which might easily be omitted, and seemed to want nature and truth of cha-

racter." That is, he agrees with Hazlitt in attributing the
merits of the comedy to the dialogue from first to last,
and to the auction and screen-scenes. And in the
dialogue Sheridan is certainly seen at his best. Though
not so humorous as in "The Rivals" he is certainly more
pointed. The level of excellence is higher and the
ornamentation more evenly arranged upon the surface
of the general structure. How Sheridan laboured over
the play we know from Moore, who shows how each scene
was cast and recast, and each phrase fashioned and re-
fashioned, until every unnecessary epithet had disappeared
and every redundant phrase had been eliminated. Moore
has been blamed for thus opening the door of Sheridan's
laboratory, but it is difficult to see why. No doubt he
destroys, to a certain extent, the reputation which
Sheridan sedulously sought to gain, that of an indolent
and careless wit. But not altogether, for we are told that
the last five scenes were dashed off on one rough draft,
and they are not markedly inferior to the rest of the
play. Sheridan, in fact, combined the methods—

"Of hasty Shadwell and slow Wycherley."

If taken at a disadvantage he was equal to the occasion,
but as a rule he was never satisfied until he had spent
himself in his efforts to secure perfection. Even so he
was barely content. When Ridgway, to whom Sheridan
had sold the copyright of the comedy, made repeated
demands for the manuscript, the dramatist told him that
he had been for nineteen years endeavouring to satisfy
himself with the style of "The School for Scandal," but

had not yet succeeded. All the more credit to him for his capacity for taking pains, for it is thus that masterpieces are made. Sheridan wrote and rewrote "The School for Scandal" just as Flaubert wrote and rewrote "Madame Bovary," and yet neither work as we have it shows much sign of the chisel. But the process by which the quarrels between Sir Peter and Lady Teazle, and the scene between Lady Teazle and Joseph Surface, were converted from indifferent imitations of Vanbrugh to excellent specimens of Sheridanese, is one of extreme interest. We learn, too, from Miss Lefanu that it was prefaced by a considerable period of "sitting and thinking." "The comedy is finished," said Sheridan; "I have now nothing to do but to write it." But even the writing was not accomplished without much experimentalizing, condensation, and refinement.

Even in its most finished state, Sheridan's art is limited, and by its limitations causes him to rank in the second not the first class of dramatists; he is a wit, but not a poet. When Hazlitt calls "The School for Scandal" the most finished and faultless comedy we have, he is surely thinking of the post-Restoration comedy. Finished it is, but hardly faultless. It would be absurd to compare the play with "As You Like It," or even with "Every Man in his Humour." Horace Walpole is quite right when he says that it is deficient in nature and truth of character. Compared with Volpone, Joseph Surface is a very crude sort of hypocrite, drawn in plain black and white, and without any nice gradations of villainy. He whips off his mask and claps it on again with the distracting abruptness of

5

a Harlequin; the fluency of his "sentiments" in the presence of Sir Peter, and the exuberance of his cynicism when plotting with Lady Sneerwell, are alike overdone. In short, Sheridan's comedy is artificial, not natural, and the touchstone of his excellence is not life, but manners. What Hazlitt has said of Congreve in his essay on the four Restoration dramatists holds equally true of his disciple and successor; and his description of the Milla-mant of "Love for Love" fits Lady Teazle, with certain reservations, to a T. Congreve, contends the prince of dramatic critics,

"has given us the finest idea of an artificial character of this kind; but it is still the reflection of an artificial character. The springs of nature, passion, or imagination are but faintly touched. The impressions appealed to, and with masterly address, are habitual, external, and conventional advantages: the ideas of birth, of fortune, of connections, of dress, accomplishment, fashion, the opinion of the world, of crowds of admirers, continually come into play, flatter our vanity, bribe our interest, fall in with our prejudices—it is these that support the goddess of our idolatry, with which she is everything, and without which she is nothing. The mere fine lady of comedy, compared with the heroine of romance or poetry, when stripped of her adventitious ornaments and advantages, is too much like the doll stripped of its finery. In thinking of Millamant we think almost as much of her dress as of her person; it is not so with Rosalind or Perdita. The poet has painted them differently; in colours which ' nature's own sweet and cunning hand laid on,' with health, with innocence, with gaiety, 'wild wit, invention ever new;' with pure red and white, like the wilding's blossoms; with warbled wood-notes, like the feathered choirs; with thoughts fluttering on the wings of imagination, and hearts panting and breathless with eager delight. The interest we feel is in themselves; the admiration they excite is for themselves. They do not depend upon the drapery of circumstances. It is nature that 'blazons herself' in them. Imogen is the same in a lonely cave as in a court; nay

more, for she there seems something heavenly—a spirit or a vision ;
and, as it were, shames her destiny, brighter for the foil of circumstances. Millamant is nothing but a fine lady ; and all her airs and
affectation would be blown away with the first breath of misfortune.
Enviable in drawing-rooms, adorable at her toilette, fashion, like a
witch, has thrown her spell about her; but if that spell were broken,
her power of fascination would be gone. For that reason I think
the character better adapted for the stage : it is more artificial,
more theatrical, more meritricious. I would rather have seen Mrs.
Abington's Millamant than any Rosalind that ever appeared on the
stage. Somehow, this sort of acquired elegance is more a thing of
costume, of air and manner ; and in comedy, or on the comic stage,
the light and familiar, the trifling, superficial, and agreeable, bears,
perhaps, rightful sway over that which touches the affections or
exhausts the fancy."

The quotation is somewhat long, but scissors and
paste may be excused where Hazlitt is concerned.
Besides, the extract helps us to formulate the true answer
to the charge so often brought against Sheridan, that his
characters are too witty, and that their wit is the same.
It is best met by a plea of guilty, combined with the
assertion that the offence committed is not a crime but
a virtue. From the artistic point of view it is no doubt
a blunder to make Trip talk like his master, and it is
inconceivable that a simple, common-place old gentleman like Sir Peter could utter the recondite witticism—
"In all cases of slander currency, whenever the drawer
of the lie was not to be found, the injured parties should
have a right to come down on any of the indorsers." So,
too, it is difficult to imagine a mere fribble, like Sir Benjamin Backbite, the perpetrator of the excellent jest about
the widow Ochre. "Come, come, 'tis not that she paints
so ill—but when she has finished her face, she joins it

on so badly to her neck, that she looks like a mended
statue, in which the connoisseur may see at once that
the head is modern, though the trunk's antique." But
when dramatic effect alone is aimed at, the more wit
there is to be found in the dialogue the better. The
object of comedy is amusement and delight, the more
its audience smile the greater its success. It is impossible
to imagine a greater intellectual treat, nor one, alas,
more unlikely of realization, than would be the performance of "Love for Love" with an adequate interpretation,
and "The School for Scandal" is not unworthy to be
ranked with "Love for Love;" for its wit, if more
laboured, is at the same time more surprising. Most of
it is Sheridan's own, but we catch, too, something of the
tones which prevailed in that by-gone age, when
Brookes's hung on the lips of Fitzpatrick, George
Selwyn, and Hare, and when Reynolds immortalized the
beauty of rank with—

> " That art, which well might added lustre give
>   To Nature's best, and Heaven's superlative :
>   On Granby's cheek might bid new glories rise,
>   Or point a purer beam from Devon's eyes." [1]

When Horace Walpole complained that "The School
for Scandal" was too long, he allowed that he was badly
posted for hearing, and the admission accounts for the
censure. Enthusiasm is apt to flag when half the sentences of a dialogue are lost. But modern audiences
are by no means inclined to yawn over the last act of

---

[1] A Portrait, addressed to Mrs. Crewe ; with the comedy of "The
School for Scandal," by R. B. Sheridan, Esq.

the play, containing, as it does, the final appearance
of Lady Sneerwell and her associates. When, however,
he complained that several of the scenes were unnecessary, he certainly hit upon what has been considered a defect in the comedy. It is pretty certain
that he alludes to the scandal-scenes proper, and they
are but loosely connected, if at all, with the main plot.
" I wish," said a first-nighter in the pit during the scene
at Lady Sneerwell's, "that these people would have
done talking and let the play begin." As Moore has
pointed out, the peculiarity is due to the fact that the
play is a combination of two distinct plots, one dealing
with the Teazles, the other with Lady Sneerwell and Sir
Benjamin Backbite as the principal personages, and not
even Sheridan's art could effect a perfect blend. But,
after all, a certain amount of digression is surely per-
missible in comedy, where the characters are not, as in
tragedy, hurried towards their doom under the compul-
sion of a relentless destiny. " Plot stood still !" exclaims Bayes in the Duke of Buckingham's " Rehearsal," " what a devil is a plot good for but to bring
in fine things !" That is an extreme view, no doubt,
but when the way is pleasant it is not culpable to loiter,
especially in the company of Sir Benjamin, Crabtree,
and Mrs. Candour. If the plot is to be everything,
and all accessories and ornamentations are to be ruth-
lessly debarred, the art of the playwright is lowered at
once to the mere ingenuity of the mechanician. But
apart from the scandal-scenes the play possesses a very
interesting and well-developed plot leading up to the
screen-scene, which is flawless. Hypercriticism has

urged that the hiding of Lady Teazle behind the screen
exposes her to the view of the maiden lady across the
way to foil whose prying eyes Joseph Surface had placed
the screen before the window. But, as Mr. Brander
Matthews has remarked, Lady Teazle rushes behind it
in her terror without consulting Joseph, and so the
objection falls to the ground.

Is "The School for Scandal" moral, or immoral, or
non moral? Hazlitt, in his Lecture, comments on the
moral value of the play, which, he says, "as often as it is
acted, must serve to clear the air of that low, creeping
fog of cant and mysticism, which threatens to confound
every native impulse or honest conviction in the
nauseous belief of a perpetual lie, and in the laudable
profession of systematic hypocrisy." But, with all due
respect to so admirable a critic, any attempt to extract
a sermon from "The School for Scandal" is beside the
point. The play is, as has been said already of "The
Rivals," purely non-moral, except for its occasional and
rather incongruous conformity with the canons of
genteel comedy. It appeals to what Charles Lamb
called the "middle emotions." The audience can, if
they like, think that a solid victory has been won by
virtue, when the hypocrisy of Joseph Surface has been
exposed, and the scandalous college has been turned
out by Sir Peter Teazle, but they are quite mistaken.
Garrick was, in his generation, wiser than they, when he
wrote in his prologue—

> " Is our young bard so young, to think that he
> Can stop the full spring-tide of calumny?

Knows he the world so little, and his trade?
Alas ! the devil's sooner raised than laid ;
So strong, so swift, the monster there's no gagging :
Cut Scandal's head off, still the tongue is wagging."

Sheridan would have answered that the devil did not come into his *scenario*, and that he appealed to the intellects not the consciences of his audience. He meant them to admire the wit of his dialogue, and appreciate the ingenuity of his plot, not to bother their heads because a full measure of poetic justice does not overtake Lady Sneerwell, and Joseph Surface does not expiate his crimes in Newgate. Both characters are purely artificial, not meant to be taken seriously, and as such they were played by the actors who learnt their parts under Sheridan's instruction.[1] Even in Charles Lamb's time the spirit of true criticism was beginning to desert theatre-goers, and he doubted if they would have endured Palmer's habit of addressing his sentiments as much to you as to Sir Peter, and King's method of playing off his "teasings" upon his audience. From the advent of the frock-coat the comic Muse had fled, and people insisted upon a realistic Joseph, with whom they could work themselves up into a fitting state of virtuous indignation. At best, as Lamb has pointed out, the character is full of incongruities, caused by Sheridan's concessions to sentimental comedy, and is one that requires to be

[1] Sheridan, however, was dissatisfied with all his Sir-Peters, from King to the elder Mathews. They were unable, says Mrs. Mathews, in her memoirs of her husband, to follow his reading of the character.

played lightly and with discretion, notably in the scene
with Sir Oliver, disguised as Old Stanley. The modern
Joseph Surface, stalking solemnly about the stage, is an
altogether tiresome person, who appears to have strayed
from some transpontine melodrama into the wrong
theatre, and to be oppressed by the fact without having
the courage to take himself off. He never rises to the full
sense of the dignity of his mission as a reformer of
morals, nor, considering that he has to pose as the
devil's advocate, is his failure altogether surprising.
Besides, it is difficult to throw intensity into a character,
who, when he has been hopelessly found out, contents
himself with the complacent remark—"Sure Fortune
never played a man of my policy such a trick before.
My character with Sir Peter, my hopes with Maria,
destroyed in a moment! I'm in a rare humour to
listen to other people's distresses! I sha'n't be able
to bestow even a benevolent sentiment on Old Stanley."
Where is the remorse, the gnawing of conscience which,
in the interests of morality, Joseph Surface should have
displayed?

Nor can the moral test be applied with any more
propriety to the characters which, for want of a better
word, must be called sympathetic—Charles Surface, Sir
Peter and Lady Teazle. All the *dramatis personæ* are
really sympathetic or unsympathetic, just as you choose
to take them, that is to say, they are untrammelled by
the domestic affections. Moore was at pains to defend
Sheridan from the charge of having damaged the
interests of honesty and virtue by the gay charm which
he has thrown round the irregularities of Charles Surface.

He does so by quoting Burke's famous phrase, that "vice loses half its evil by losing all its grossness," and exalts Charles at the expense of the rakes of Congreve and Farquhar. But the volatile and spendthrift hero of "The School for Scandal," despite his regard for his absent uncle and his generosity towards Old Stanley, is not conceived with any more serious purport than the Roebuck of Farquhar's "Love and a Bottle." The contrast between his open-handed recklessness and the the sentimental hypocrisy of Joseph is an effective stage-contrast, and nothing more, and is to be judged neither by copybook texts nor the Duty towards my Neighbours. It is stage-virtue which triumphs and stage-vice which is defeated, but though we are glad that all ends happily, there is no "Go thou and do like-wise" in the matter at all. It is the fashion to talk about the elevating influence of the stage and its capacity for handling social problems, yet there is not much profit to be derived from plays professing to deal with problems social or moral, nor anything but weariness and nausea from a medical blue-book of the Ibsen class. But to read or hear a good comedy, such as Sheridan's masterpiece, is, to use Hazlitt's phrase, "to keep the best company in the world, where the best things are said, and the most amusing happen." It is not life, but a relief from life, with its appointments, its work, and its butchers' bills. If we became acquainted with Lady Teazle in society we should be outraged by the brutality of her desire to become a widow, and when we discovered that she had voluntarily returned to Joseph Surface's house, in which she had been a few

hours previously on the brink of transgression, we should
look upon her as a brazen baggage.   But on the stage
these incongruities only appear in a half light, and she
remains a purely delightful and irresponsible creature.
Similarly, it is possible to feel a sense of genuine satisfaction, when Sir Peter escapes cuckoldry, without caring
whether his indignation is at all adequate to the occasion.
From the moralist's point of view a husband who in a
similar situation thinks only of the ridicule which will
fall upon himself is a somewhat contemptible person ;
and Sir Peter's reconciliation with his wife would be
set down as dictated by uxoriousness rather than
magnimity.   But somehow it is impossible to conceive
Sir Peter Teazle as other than a thoroughly estimable
and simple-minded old gentleman.   In real life how
terrible must have been his discomfiture on the fall of
the screen, and how heartless would the speech of
Charles have sounded.   The scene is frequently acted
as if it were tragedy, and then it becomes simply absurd.
Garrick saw that any expression of genuine emotion
would ruin it at once.

"A gentleman," he wrote to Sheridan on the 12th of May, "who
is as mad as myself about ye School remarked, that the characters
upon the stage at ye falling of the screen stand too long before they
speak. I thought so too ye first night—tho' they should be astonish'd
and a little petrify'd, yet it may be carry'd to too great a length."

Off the stage a good deal of astonishment would
surely have been legitimate on such an occasion, but
Garrick knew, what many of Sheridan's critics have not
known, that comedy has laws of its own.   Its merit may
not be in proportion to its unreality, but it can have little

merit if it be real, for the average incidents and the average conversations of life are but poor comedy.

It remains to deal with the charges of plagiarism which have been brought against this, as against the other plays of Sheridan. On the whole, they may be said at once to amount to a hint borrowed from one source and another, and to nothing more. And though plagiarism is not, as Ben Jonson contended, meritorious in itself, Sheridan at least could claim that nearly everything he appropriated from others was improved by the process. Dr. Watkins, indeed, in his scissors-and-paste biography of Sheridan, was good enough to hint that "The School for Scandal" was not Sheridan's at all, but the work either of Mrs. Sheridan or of an anonymous young lady, who died of consumption at Bristol Hot-wells. Moore, whether advisedly or no, destroyed this comically foolish myth by printing extract after extract from Sheridan's rough drafts, demonstrating thereby the intellectual labour by which the comedy was built up. Sheridan himself, it may be noted, never condescended to meet this and similar accusations except by a little genial banter in "The Critic."

"*Dangle.* Sir Fretful, have you sent your play to the managers yet? or can I be of any service to you?

"*Sir Fretful.* No, no, I thank you; I believe the piece had sufficient recommendation with it. I thank you though. I sent it to the manager of COVENT GARDEN THEATRE this morning.

"*Sneer.* I should have thought now that it might have been cast (as the actors call it) better at DRURY LANE.

"*Sir Fretful.* O, lud, no!—never send a play there while I live. Hark'ee! (*whispers Sneer.*)

"*Sneer.* Writes himself! I know he does!

"*Sir Fretful.* I say nothing. I take away from no man's merit. Am hurt at no man's good fortune. I say nothing. But this I will say, through all my knowledge of life, I have discovered that there is not a passion so strongly rooted in the human breast as envy.

"*Sneer.* I believe you have reason for what you say, indeed.

"*Sir Fretful.* Besides, I can tell you it is not always so safe to leave a play in the hands of those who write themselves.

"*Sneer.* What! they may steal from them, hey, my dear Plagiary?

"*Sir Fretful.* Steal! to be sure they may, and egad! serve your best thoughts as gipsies do stolen children, disfigure them to make 'em pass for their own.

"*Sneer.* But your present work is a sacrifice to Melpomene, and HE you know never——

"*Sir Fretful.* That's no security—a dexterous plagiarist may do anything. Why, Sir, for aught I know, he might take out some of the best things in my tragedy and put them into his own comedy."

This was answer enough; and as to the actual genesis of "The School for Scandal," we are informed by Miss Lefanu that Sheridan conceived the idea of dealing with the subject on perusing the wild legends current in the Bath papers after his second duel with Captain Mathews. The statement is borne out by Moore's evidence that the scandalous college was, in the first sketch of the play, established in the Pump Room at Bath, and Crabtree may after all have been drawing upon the imagination of some journalist, not his own, when he described how—

"Charles' shot took effect, as I tell you, and Sir Peter's missed; but, what is very extraordinary, the ball struck against a little bronze Shakespeare that stood over the fire-place, grazed out of the window at a right angle, and wounded the postman, who was just coming to the door with a double letter from Northamptonshire."

But scandal, like most of the other failings of mankind,

had already been made the subject of satire, and
Sheridan was not above taking a hint from his predecessors in his management of the theme. We can
trace the scandal-scenes properly so-called of "The
School" through three generations. The first is the scene
in the "Misanthrope" of Molière, where Célimène dis-
cusses her acquaintance. Then we have a short scene in
Wycherley's "Plain Dealer" (act ii. scene 1), in which
Novel and Olivia talk over the people with whom Novel
had been dining. From the latter play Sheridan seems
to have borrowed one or two suggestions : for instance,
Joseph Surface's ironical compliment to Mrs. Candour
on her forbearance and good nature, and Lady Sneerwell's description of Mrs. Evergreen. To Congreve's
"Double-Dealer" (act iii. scene 10), Sheridan was even
more indebted, and it can hardly be said that his wit
materially improves that of the original. Indeed, Sir
Benjamin Backbite's verse must be pronounced inferior
in drollery to Lady Froth's admirable effusion :—

> " For as the sun shines every day,
> So of our coachman I may say,
> He shows his drunken fiery face
> Just as the sun does more or less."

Again, the comments of Lady Sneerwell, Mrs.
Candour, and Sir Benjamin upon their absent friends,
though more elaborate than those of Lady Froth and
Brisk, are not, *pace* Moore, a whit more pointed. And
Sheridan has lessened the dramatic effect of the whole
scene, as Mr. Gosse, in his monograph on Congreve has
pointed out, by making Lady Teazle join in the destruc-

tion of reputations, instead of imitating Cynthia in her
expression of disgust at the whole proceeding.   Nor do
the two scandal-scenes exhaust the points of resemblance
between "The School for Scandal" and "The Double-
Dealer."   Joseph Surface's relations with Lady Teazle
and Maria are very similar to those between Maskwell,
Lady Touchwood, and Cynthia, though Congreve pro-
vides an additional complication by making Lady Touchwood in love with Mellefont, the Charles Surface of the
piece, who it may be noted has a friend called Careless.
Lady Touchwood, in fact, combines the functions of
Lady Teazle and Lady Sneerwell.   But it is pretty certain that the resemblance is accidental, since we know
that "The School for Scandal," as we have it, is an
amalgamation of two distinct plots, conceived inde-
pendently, and therefore not derived from a common
source.   All that can be said is, that when Sheridan
decided on joining his plots together he may possibly
have seen that the characters lent themselves to a
dénouement something similar to Congreve's.   If so, the
origin of the screen-scene is to be discovered, not, as the
over-ingenious Boaden suggested, in the exposure of
Square though the fall of a rug in Molly Seagrim's bedroom, but in the elaborate intrigue in the fourth and
fifth acts of "The Double-Dealer," which brings Maskwell, Mellefont, Lord and Lady Touchwood together in
Lady Touchwood's chamber, with the result that Lord
Touchwood's eyes are opened to the villainy of Maskwell.

The remainder of Sheridan's indebtedness may be
briefly dismissed.   It has been said that Charles and

Joseph Surface are copied from Fielding's Tom Jones
and Blifil, and Joseph Surface has also been traced to
Molière and to the Malvil of Arthur Murphy's " Know
your own Mind." It was quite possible that the contrast
between Charles and Joseph may have been immediately
suggested to Sheridan by Fielding; but it is old enough
in all conscience, and if Sheridan did not go to sleep in
church he must frequently have heard the story of Esau
and Jacob. Strange it is that Sheridan's critics should
have failed to see that the very fact that Joseph Surface can be traced to so many sources proves that he
can owe very little to any of them. A play must have
a bad man in it, otherwise it becomes insipid and un-
dramatic, and assassins being out of place in comedy,
hypocrites are almost indispensable. Tartuffe and Joseph
Surface are both hypocrites, but there the resemblance
ends. As to the Malvil theory, which has the authority
of Hazlitt, it is more tenable. But all that can safely be
asserted is that Sheridan may have seen the play—it was
produced at Covent Garden on February 22, 1777—
while he was writing " The School for Scandal." From
a solitary sentence uttered by Malvil, " To a person of
sentiment like you, madam, a visit is paid with pleasure,"
Sheridan may have conceived the idea of making Joseph
Surface a sententious hypocrite, but otherwise the two
characters have nothing in common beyond being
hypocrites. Old Sheridan once made a remark which,
though it was given an uncomplimentary turn, probably contained a good deal of truth. " Talk of the
merit of Dick's comedy," said he, " there's nothing in
it. He had but to dip the pencil in his own heart,

and he'd find there the characters both of Joseph and
Charles " — that is, his father, in his most censorious
mood, thought them original creations.

Again, it is quite possible that Sheridan may, as Boaden
suggested, have borrowed from his mother's novel, "Miss
Sidney Biddulph," the incident of the arrival of Sir
Oliver from India, and his visit to his relations in disguise.　The loan is a trivial one, hardly more considerable than the name of Surface which was taken from her
comedy, "A Trip to Bath."　So, too, the idea of
"little Premium" may have been taken from the "little
Transfer the broker," of Foote's "Minor," and Rowley
is neither the first nor the last of the faithful stewards
who have trod the stage of comedy.　None of these
appropriations matters in the least when compared with
the manner in which it is used ; and none is incompatible with a due respect to tradition.　If plagiarism is
made the sole test of literary merit, we may well
exclaim with the Scotchman in the pit at the first
representation of Home's "Douglas," "Whar's Wullie
Shakespeare noo ? "　But a lack of originality in minor
details is as dust in the balance, if the treatment and
style of the whole be excellent.　They are the only
true touchstones, and it is by them "The School for
Scandal" must be judged.　If they are applied, "The
School for Scandal," even when placed by the side of
"Love for Love," or "The Way of the World," must
be pronounced a great comedy, with an adequate plot,
several perfect scenes, and a dialogue of consummate
brilliance and polish.　As literature it may not be equal
to Congreve, but as acted drama it is far superior.

CHAPTER V.

IN spite of the complete triumph of "The School for Scandal," there seems to have been still a good deal of uncertainty about the fortunes of Drury Lane. Garrick was at first sanguine. "This is but a single play," observed a critic, "and in the long run will be but a slender help to support the theatre. To you, Mr. Garrick, I must say the Atlas that propped the stage has left his station." "Has he?" said Garrick; "if that be the case he has found another Hercules to succeed him." But soon afterwards, on July 13, 1777, we find him writing to King: "Poor old Drury! it will, I fear, very soon be in the hand of the Philistines." And Mrs. Clive, though long retired from the stage, was evidently well posted in theatrical news, for she wrote to the great actor in the following year: "Everybody is raving against Mr. Sheridan for his supineness; there never was such a contrast as between Garrick and Sheridan; what have you given him that he creeps so?" To make matters worse, old Sheridan, whom in an evil hour his son had appointed stage manager, by way of sealing their long-delayed reconciliation, contrived, through his

6

ridiculous self-importance, to pick a quarrel with Garrick, who wrote indignantly :—

"Pray assure your father that I meant not to interfere in his department. I imagined (foolishly indeed) my attending Bannister's rehearsal of the part I once played, and which your father never saw [Zaphna], might have assisted the cause without giving the least offence. I love my ease too well to be thought an interloper, and I should not have been impertinent enough to have attended any rehearsal had not you, Sir, in a very particular manner, desired me. However, upon no consideration will I ever interfere again in this business, nor be liable to receive such another message as was brought to me this evening by young Bannister."

The letter is undated, but it was probably written in October, 1778,[1] and on January 20, 1779, David Garrick died. Sheridan was chief mourner at his funeral, and wrote a monody to his memory, which was recited by Mrs. Yates on the 2nd of March, at Drury Lane. It is Sheridan's longest essay in poetry, and certainly his least successful. The metre is correct, and there is a fine line or two, but the whole is monotonous. In fact, the heroic couplet taken seriously was beyond Sheridan. Again, in his treatment of the subject there is much to be desired. Sheridan used to declare that he had never seen Garrick act, and the statement was probably put forward as an excuse for the fact that there is not an attempt throughout the poem to recall the peculiar genius of the great comedian, whom most of those present must have remembered so well. Instead, they had to put up with elaborate commonplaces on the fugitive nature of

[1] The play was called "Mahomet," and it was produced on October 11th.

the actor's art and fame, a thought which, as Moore well
remarks, had already been more simply expressed by
Garrick himself in his prologue to "The Clandestine
Marriage." The best passage in the poem owed its
inspiration to a saying of Burke's over the grave,
which in Sheridan's hands became—

> " The throng that mourn'd as their dead favourite pass'd,
> The grac'd respect that claim'd him to the last ;
> *While Shakespeare's image, from its hallow'd base,*
> *Seem'd to prescribe the grave, and point the place.*"

During all these months Sheridan's pen lay idle. The
public chose indeed to attribute to him an indifferent
trifle called "The Camp," which was produced in October, 1778. But it was really by his friend Tickell, and
Sheridan, out of sheer good nature, allowed the rumour
to go uncontradicted. Many people besides Mrs. Clive
were probably angry with him for his indolence, but
"The School for Scandal" continued to draw good
houses, and the company having been strengthened by
the accession of Henderson, who was seen at his best in
tragedy, Shakespearian revivals were of frequent occur-
rence. Sheridan, then, had more than one excuse for
resting on his oars, and of them he was, in all probability,
only too glad to avail himself. At length he resumed his
activity, and set to work on " The Critic," his last genuine
play, which was brought out on October 30, 1779.
Though the farce was evidently written with the utmost
care, Sheridan as usual could not be induced to finish it
until the last moment. Two days before it was announced,
the final scene had not been written, but the combined

intelligences of Linley and King were equal to the occasion.   Linley decoyed Sheridan down to the theatre, and
King locked him into the green-room, with the prompter's
unfinished copy of "The Critic," writing materials, two
bottles of claret, and a dish of anchovy sandwiches.   He
was told that he was to finish the wine and the farce, but
was to consider himself a prisoner until they were both
at an end.   Sheridan laughed and obeyed.

According to a familiar story, "The Critic" was written
to repay Cumberland for his conduct on the first night of
" The School for Scandal."   It was said that the captious
author took his children to the play, and when they
screamed with delight he pinched them, exclaiming,
" What are you laughing at, my dear little folks?   You
should not laugh, my angels, there is nothing to laugh
at !" and then in an undertone, " Keep still, you little
dunces !"   When Sheridan was told of this, he is reported
to have said, " Devilish ungrateful that, for I sat out his
tragedy last week, and laughed from beginning to end."
The anecdote is good, but unfortunately it will not bear
investigation.   Cumberland's first tragedy, "The Battle
of Hastings," was not produced until 1778, the year after
" The School for Scandal," and in his Memoirs he denies
the whole story, declaring that he was at Bath at the
time, and that he did not see the play at all during its
first run.   There can be no doubt, however, that Sir
Fretful Plagiary was intended for Cumberland, and
many passages in his Memoirs attest the accuracy of the
portrait.   So too Dangle, who is concisely described by
Mrs. Dangle as "a mock Mæcenas to second-hand
authors," is said to have been a caricature of one

Vaughan. If this is the " Hat " Vaughan who befriended Sheridan during his last days, he took a very noble revenge.

As a matter of fact the travesty of a rehearsal, the sub-ject of " The Critic," was new neither to Sheridan nor to the stage, and Sir Fretful Plagiary and Dangle were evidently afterthoughts. We have seen that a burlesque called " Jupiter," written in conjunction with Halhed, was one of his earliest dramatic efforts, and Moore tells us that the form of a rehearsal into which the whole was thrown, was suggested and arranged entirely by Sheridan. The character of Simile in the boyish attempt is clearly a rough draft of our friend Puff. Besides, the repro-duction and improvement of old material is entirely characteristic of Sheridan. He even adapted, and in-serted in his pieces, the love-poems addressed to his wife. But if Sheridan reproduced in " The Critic " a plan which had been already attempted by himself, he also reproduced a plan which had been attempted many times by earlier dramatic authors, since Fletcher had set the fashion by his " Knight of the Burning Pestle." By far the most successful of these efforts was the Duke of Buckingham's " The Rehearsal," written to ridicule Dryden under the character of Bayes. Latterly Fielding had tried the same scheme in a variety of plays, of which " Pasquin " was the most meritorious. Sheridan could, then, hardly lay claim to originality of design; but it is absurd to dismiss " The Critic," as did Horace Walpole, with the remark that it was " wondrously old and flat; a poor imitation."

For here, again, the charges of plagiarism brought

against Sheridan are very inconclusive; the model was old, but the treatment was almost entirely his own. A phrase or two exhausts his indebtedness to Fielding, and his borrowings from the Duke of Buckingham are hardly more considerable. They are confined to the play rehearsed, "The Spanish Armada," and the only loans that are at all obvious are Mr. Puff's announcement of his grand scene, "Now then for my magnificence, my battle, my noise, and my procession !" and the opening words of Sir Christopher Hatton, "True, gallant Raleigh," with Dangle's query, "What, they had been talking before ?" and Puff's reply, "Oh, yes ; all the way as they came along." Otherwise Bayes has little in common with Puff, beyond being a dramatic author, and he resembles Sir Fretful Plagiary only in keeping a common-place book, into which he conveys other people's ideas. But so it is to be presumed do most plagiarists. And, Sheridan, as always, improved upon his predecessors. Not that "The Rehearsal" does not contain many excellent points. In particular, the eclipse formed by a dance in which three actors representing the sun, moon, and earth, change places, is quite as good as, if not better than, Sheridan's Thames with his two banks on one side. But, as a whole, it is diffuse and too evidently written to satisfy the spleen of the moment by ridiculing Dryden's personal peculiarities. Sheridan's Dangle, Sir Fretful Plagiary, and Puff, on the other hand, are types which even at this distance of time have not lost their vitality, though two, if not the third, were intended to satirise individuals. The first act in which Mr. Puff developes the art of puffing, contains some of Sheridan's very best comedy.

Fanny Burney, when she read it, decided that it was "as full of wit, satire, and spirit, as of lines." It is never acted now except in a mangled form. But one can well imagine how the audiences of 1779 must have enjoyed King's clear delivery of the description of the "puff direct," especially when he gave vent to an eloquent panegyric on Dodd (Dangle), Palmer (Sneer), and himself :—

"Mr. Dodd was astonishingly great in the character of Sir Harry. That universal and judicious actor, Mr. Palmer, perhaps never appeared to more advantage than in the colonel; but it is not in the power of language to do justice to Mr. King: indeed, he more than merited those frequent bursts of applause which he drew from a most brilliant and judicious audience."

Incidentally, too, the first act of "The Critic" is important as containing Sheridan's valedictory remarks on sentimental comedy, which he had killed by the success of his own plays. They are rather severe.

"*Dangle* [reading]. *Bursts into tears and exit.* What is this; a tragedy?

"*Sneer.* No, that's a genteel comedy, not a translation—only taken from the French; it is written in a style which they have lately tried to run down; the true sentimental, and nothing ridiculous from the beginning to the end.

"*Mrs. Dangle.* Well, if they had kept to that, I should not have been such an enemy to the stage; there is some edification to be got out of those pieces, Mr. Sneer.

"*Sneer.* I am quite of your opinion, Mrs. Dangle: the theatre, in proper hands, might certainly be made the school of morality; but now, I am sorry to say it, people seem to go there principally for their entertainment!"

If the comedy of the first act of "The Critic" has

stood the wear and tear of time, so has the satire of the
second act. The particular plays at which it was aimed,
such as Home's " Fatal Discovery," have long since
become obsolete, and have had but few successors. For
" The Critic " killed bombastic tragedy much as " The
School for Scandal" killed sentimental comedy.
" Zorayda," which was brought out immediately afterwards, was withdrawn after a run of eight nights, as its
heroine was found to have been forestalled by Tilburnia.
But " The Spanish Armada " is a burlesque of bad plays
in general, quite as much as bad tragedies individually.
So long as convention rules the drama, conversations will
be overheard under the most improbable circumstances,
under-plots will continue to have but little connection
with main-plots, and heroines will go mad, though no
longer in white satin. And until all sense of humour has
been eliminated from English life, people will quote and
laugh at " No scandal about Queen Elizabeth, I hope,"
"The Spanish fleet thou can'st not see—because It is
not yet in sight," and " Where they do agree upon the
stage, their unanimity is wonderful."

With " The Critic," Sheridan's literary and dramatic
productions came, practically speaking, to an end. He
was still ready to help an acquaintance, for instance, by
writing the lively epilogue to Hannah More's play, " The
Fatal Falsehood," and the prologue to Lady Craven's
" Miniature Picture," which was eventually transferred
to " Pizarro." But even so far as poetry was concerned,
he was content to shine in ladies' albums, and the fragments which Moore found among his papers were
unimportant. Shortly after his death there appeared

under his name an "Ode to Scandal," which, if it be really his, is as good as any verse he ever wrote.[1] It has been included as Sheridan's in more than one poetical anthology. But its genuineness appears to be quite an open question. Moore never so much as mentions it, though he must have known of its existence, and though in writing Sheridan's life he was, as may be seen in his diary, often at a loss for materials. Again it was sent anonymously to the publisher, Wright, of Fleet Street, accompanied by a letter of Sheridan's which, as it is not given by Wright, evidently had nothing to do with the Ode. Wright says, indeed, in his advertisement to the public, that he was sure of the quarter whence the Ode came; but was he likely to have been particularly scrupulous, when the supposed author could no longer bring him to book? Internal evidence also points to the conclusion that the Ode is not Sheridan's. The metre is far more elaborate than any he was accustomed to use,

---

[1] As the "Ode to Scandal" has been seldom republished, an extract from it may be given here :

> " The first informations
> Of lost reputations
> As offerings to thee I'll consign ;
> And the earliest news
> Of surprised billet-doux
> Shall constant be served at thy shrine.
> Intrigues by the score
> Never heard of before
> Shall the sacrifice daily augment,
> And by each *Morning Post*
> Some favourite toast
> A victim to thee shall be sent."

and the poem, so far from being as the publisher impu-
dently suggested, the origin of " The School for Scandal,"
does not contain a single anticipation of that play.
Possibly the Ode, like a good deal of pseudo-Sheridan
work, may have been Tickell's.

Sheridan's subsequent contributions to the drama were
not of much greater consequence. He applied the
pruning-knife, as we shall see, to " The Stranger,"
and adapted the adaptation of " Pizarro." He even
sketched out the plot of " The Glorious First of June,"
and of two spectacular pieces, the " Forty Thieves" and
the pantomime, " Robinson Crusoe," in the last of which
pieces of pot-boiling he was accused by the clown
Delpini of having stolen from him the joke of pulling off
a man's leg together with his boot. But from dramatic
authorship of a more elevated character he instinctively
recoiled. No doubt his time was much taken up
by politics, society, and the routine of management.
But it is clear also that he recognized that in " The .
School for Scandal" he had reached his zenith, and
feared the risk of a temporary failure, perhaps of a
gradual decline. Two unfinished plays, or sketches of
plays, were found among his papers by Moore. The first
in its original form was a musical drama, without a name,
but evidently founded on " The Goblings" of Sir John
Suckling, since its chief personages were a band of out-
laws in the guise of Devils. It was left very incomplete,
and all that can be said of it is that it was apparently
written subsequently to his residence at Bath. From
this unnamed play was evolved an opera-book, called
" The Foresters." Of this piece Moore could only dis-

cover a fragment or two, but the anonymous Octogenarian who subsequently published some loose memoirs of Sheridan, declared that at least two acts were finished, and that the piece was undertaken just after his second marriage, that is, in 1795. Far more to be regretted is his abandonment of his projected comedy of "Affectation," which never progressed beyond a few sketches of character, many embryo jokes, and the christening of three of the intended personages—Sir Babble Bore, Sir Peregrine Paradox, and Feignwit. Evidently he failed to hit upon an interesting plot in which to set the characters, and though Sir Peter Teazle's opinion of them would have been worth listening to, Sheridan had the example of Vanbrugh's comparative failure in "Sir Henry Wildair," to warn him against a sequel to "The School for Scandal." He certainly wished it to be believed that he was hard at work on both plays. "Wait," he used to say, smilingly, "until you have seen my 'Foresters;'" and from time to time the "puff preliminary" appeared in the papers, announcing the approaching completion both of "The Foresters" and of "Affectation." But those who knew him well never believed that either play would ever see the light. Michael Kelly said to him one day, "You will never write again; you are afraid to write." Sheridan fixed his penetrating eye on Kelly, and asked, "Of whom am I afraid?" Kelly retorted, "You are afraid of the author of 'The School for Scandal.'" If Kelly really made the remark, and did not merely improve in his Reminiscences upon a similar saying of Garrick's, it was very clever of him.

CHAPTER VI.

AT the close of 1779 Sheridan commanded a source
of income which, fluctuating though it might be,
must have seemed to a person of his sanguine disposition
well-nigh inexhaustible. Now was the time for realizing
what had probably been from the first the main object of
his ambition—a reputation as a statesman. It is clear
that all along he intended literary fame to be merely
a stepping-stone to political renown. The stage of the
House of Commons appealed to a larger audience than
that of Drury Lane, and he hoped, no doubt, to supple-
ment the revenue derived from the theatre by the salary
of office. It was an age of political adventurers, most
of them, remarkably enough, of Anglo-Irish parentage.
Burke had preceded Sheridan, Tierney and Canning
were to follow him. They, one and all, won their way
to great positions, but about all of them there hung the
suspicion that a man who makes politics a trade, is to be
used rather than trusted. Sheridan, in particular, never
attained a status higher than the second rank, though
his capacities were of the highest. Indeed his oppor-
tunities of ministerial distinction of any sort were
remarkably few, since he was condemned to serve under

a leader whose blundering tactics condemned the Whig party to year after year of opposition. It was not very long before Mrs. Sheridan, at any rate, discovered that the pursuit of politics was having a disastrous effect upon her husband's circumstances. " I am more than ever convinced," she wrote to him in 1790, "we must look to other resources for wealth and independence, and consider politics merely as an amusement." The theatre suffered from the scanty time that Sheridan was able to bestow upon it, and the chance of Fox's return to power became more and more remote. But when Sheridan resolved on embracing a political career the prospects of the Whigs were far rosier. Lord North's star was obviously setting, Pitt's had not yet risen, and the Opposition were confident of a speedy return to office. Everything combined to urge him to lay down his pen, and mount the hustings.

Youth is generally in antagonism to the powers that be. Besides, Sheridan's political friendships were chiefly among the assailants of Lord North's ministry. He had formed the acquaintance of Mr. Windham at Bath; he met Burke at the Turk's Head Club, and the intimacy was continued at the Literary Club. To Fox he was introduced by Lord John Townshend, and a mutual admiration ensued. It would be interesting if we could fix the date of the acquaintances. But it is impossible to do so with exactitude. So far back as August, 1777, we find Lord Camden writing to Garrick that Fox had marked Sheridan down as the first genius of his time. Fox must presumably have arrived at the conclusion after their first interview, from which he rose with the remark that he had always thought Hare, after Charles Town-shend, the wittiest man he ever met with, but that Sheridan surpassed them both infinitely. Under these auspices his pen was readily enlisted on the side of the Opposition. Of his earlier efforts, however, an answer to Dr. Johnson's "Taxation no Tyranny," perished stillborn, and an "Essay on Irish Absentees" never advanced beyond a rough draft. He now became a contributor to *The Englishman*, a periodical in which Lord North's administration was held up to the scorn and opprobrium of mankind. Like most men of Irish extraction, Sheri-dan was a born journalist, and a paper in which the Premier was compared to the "most poor, *credulous* monster" of "The Tempest" may possibly have annoyed even Lord North's amiability, though it is equally possible that he did not take the trouble to read the lampoon.

Election to Brookes's Club, effected, if Wraxall may be trusted, in spite of the determined blackballing of George Selwyn and Lord Bessborough, converted Sheri-dan into a full-blown Whig, and at the general election of 1780 he was returned for Stafford. At the same time William Wilberforce was returned for Hull ; and William Pitt, after unsuccessfully canvassing Cambridge, was brought in shortly afterwards for Appleby. It is well known that Sheridan's maiden speech was something like a failure, but his depression was of short duration, and he anticipated young Benjamin Disraeli by exclaiming to Woodfall, "It is in me, however, and, by God, it shall come out." However, he seems to have recognized that the House was not to be taken by storm, and for several sessions intervened but rarely in debate. Indeed his position was none of the most encouraging. He had no powerful borough-monger at his back, and his connection with the stage was resented by more than one member of that fastidious assembly. Thus Mr. Courtenay, "Lord No th's deputy buffoon," accused him of not being able to endure wit in any house except his own; and even after he had been advanced to ministerial rank, a young prig named William Pitt, recommended him to confine his abilities to their proper stage—*sui plausu gaudere theatri.* The reply was wonderfully happy.

" Flattered and encouraged by the Right Honourable Gentleman's panegyric on my talents, if ever I again engage in the composition he alludes to, I may be tempted to an act of presumption—to attempt an improvement on one of Ben Jonson's best characters, the character of the Angry Boy in the ' Alchemist.' "

Compelled to fight mainly for his own hand, Sheridan won his way by what Wraxall terms "a sort of fascina-tion." To an insuperable command of temper was added that rare style of wit which is always appropriate and never offensive. Though nearly every sitter on the Government benches was exposed in turn to the sting of his satire, none of them ever had an excuse for calling him out. How, for instance, could a luckless pedant pick a quarrel with Sheridan when he began his reply to a speech full of classical quotations with—Τὸν δ'ἀπομει-βόμενος προσέφη Sheridanios ἥρως ? [1]

[1] This version of the story has the authority of De Quincey ("Selections Grave and Gay," vol. ii. p. 41). Another version is that when the speaker, Lord Belgrave, had finished, Sheridan rose and declared that if the noble Lord had proceeded a little further and completed the quotation, he would have seen that it pointed

Though Sheridan took but little part in the debates on American affairs, which were the chief topic of discussion during the last years of Lord North's luckless ministry, he rapidly became an important member of the Whig party. In 1781 he was chosen to propose a motion against the employment of the military in the suppression of the Gordon Riots; and in the following year, when Lord North finally succumbed, was appointed Under-

the other way. He then proceeded to rattle off, *ore rotundo*, a sentence of bogus Greek, the *ais* and *ois* of which completely took in Lord Belgrave, the House, and even Charles Fox, excellent scholar though he was. The second story is evidently an exaggeration of the first, and it may be that all that really happened was that Lord Belgrave misquoted, and Sheridan set him right. This view is borne out by some lines of Sheridan's, communicated to *Notes and Queries* of April, 1863, by " B.S.," evidently a member of the Sheridan family. They will be readily recognized as part of the series in which occurs the well-known verse —

> " Johnny Wilkes, Johnny Wilkes,
> Thou greatest of bilks," &c.

The lines are —

> " Lord Belgrave, Lord Belgrave,
> Why look you so hellgrave,
> And why do you seldom now speak?
> Have the damned Sunday papers
> Giv'n your Lordship the vapours (a)
> Or are you rev'sing your Greek,
>   Lord Belgrave,
> Or are you revising your Greek ? " (b)

(a) *Vide* his Lordship's methodistical language in support of Mr. Wilberforce's motion to suppress the Sunday papers.

(b) See Debrett's reports of a celebrated Greek misquotation of his Lordship's.

Secretary of State to his friend Fox. He had, however, but little chance of distinguishing himself before the death of the Prime Minister, the Marquis of Rockingham, broke up the administration. When Lord Shelburne, "the Jesuit of Berkeley Square," accepted the office of first Lord of the Treasury, for which he had long been intriguing, Sheridan followed Fox into opposition. The step was a most disinterested one on the part of a lesser placeman, inasmuch as the majority of the Cabinet adhered to Shelburne, but Sheridan summed up the situation in a bright sentence : " Those who go are right, for there is really no other question but whether, having lost their power, they ought to stay and lose their characters." Unfortunately for their credit, the friends of Mr. Fox were not content to form an isolated Opposition, but, throwing themselves into the arms of Lord North, formed that coalition against Lord Shelburne upon which the verdict of history is one of merited, if somewhat exaggerated, condemnation. To Sheridan's sound common sense a union of parties, made in defiance of public opinion and past professions, seemed a proceeding fraught with danger, and he expostulated with his headstrong leader. " It is as fixed," was Fox's reply, "as the Hanover succession." [1]

Nothing but success, as Fox owned, could justify the

[1] Lord John Townshend, writing many years afterwards, *i.e.*, in 1830, declared that Sheridan was most anxious for the Coalition, and that it was not until it failed that he began to declaim against it (Lord John Russell's " Memorials and Correspondence of C. J. Fox," vol. ii. p. 24). The tone of Sheridan's speeches, however, during his tenure of office supports the view taken in the text—that is, if the versions given by Wraxall can be relied upon.

Coalition, and success was not to be theirs. At first, however, they seemed practically invincible, and Sheridan, now Secretary to the Treasury, rendered them valuable service in debate through his readiness of tongue. " He improved daily in speech," wrote Horace Walpole, "turning all the Opposition said into excellent ridicule, and always brought the House into good humour with the Ministers." There seems to have been some sort of promise that on the first re-arrangement of the Cabinet, he should be made Chancellor of the Exchequer; but whatever hopes he may have cherished were cut short when the king, taking advantage of the clamour excited by Fox's India Bill, induced the House of Lords by a personal canvass to throw out the obnoxious measure, and then ordered the ministers to deliver up their seals of office. The rout of the Opposition at the general election, which followed Pitt's assumption of power in the teeth of a Parliamentary majority, was complete. Sheridan however managed to escape being one of " Fox's Martyrs," after expending over two thousand pounds on his election, with items—ale tickets, £40 ; subscription to clergymen's widows, £2 2s.

In the Parliament of 1784, Pitt was entirely master of the situation. Nearly 160 of the Opposition failed to re-appear, and on the new India Bill Mr. Fox only obtained a minority of 60 against a majority of 271. With a caution beyond his years the Prime Minister refrained from pressing heroic measures upon his supporters, who were for the most part reactionaries of the type of Mr. Rolle, the hero of the " Rolliad," and during the next few sessions schemes of financial reform, cautiously conceived and modestly introduced, were the topics of discussion. Sheridan, on the strength of his experience as Secretary to the Treasury, was put forward as the Opposition critic. Though Moore retails a somewhat absurd story about his qualifying himself for the post of honour by four days' study of arithmetic, there is no real reason why Sheridan should not have been quite as competent an authority on money matters as any other of Fox's followers, with the exception of Burke. Ignorance of finance was supreme on the Opposition benches. Fox himself confessed that he did not know why the Funds went up or down, and Lord John Cavendish, who had presided over the Exchequer in the Rockingham and Coalition ministries, was, for the time being, out of Parliament. Such criticism as Sheridan could offer, however, was practically valueless. He played round questions rather than attacked them directly, and failed alike to detect the merits of the commercial treaty with France, or the demerits of the sinking fund. At the same time he very nearly exposed the fallacy upon which that famous expedient was founded. Pitt, he declared, might say with the person in the comedy, "If you won't lend me the money, how can I pay you?" Even more shortsighted was the support given by him to the clamour raised by the English merchants against Pitt's measure for establishing commercial equality between England and Ireland. Sheridan loved his country, but his advocacy of her interests was not always well-advised. It was that of a fighting politician, not of a statesman.

As a relief to dull debates on financial and administrative reform, came in 1786 the impeachment of Warren Hastings. The indictment of the ex-Governor-General, as every schoolboy knows, had long been determined upon by Burke; it was precipitated by the indiscretion of Hastings' supporter, Major Scott. In April the charges were laid before the House, and the leaders of the Opposition proceeded to show cause for moving for an impeachment. After Burke had dealt with the Rohilla War, and Fox with Cheyte Singh, came the prorogation. Of the merits of that great and intricate case it is unnecessary to say further here than that in spite of much exaggeration on the part of Hastings' accusers, there can be no doubt that on more than one point they proved their charges up to the hilt. Yet Hastings saved an empire by his exactions from the native princes, and if ever the end justified the means, it did so in his case. However, such considerations are only too apt to go to the wall when a question is made one of party, and so far as Sheridan was concerned it is only due to him to say that of all the gravamina laid at the Governor-General's door, his conduct towards the Begums of Oude is the least defensible. This charge Sheridan made his own, and on February 7, 1787, delivered a speech which was universally regarded as one of the most magnificent displays of oratory that had ever been exhibited.[1]

[1] It is perhaps unnecessary to point out, at this time of day, the thorough wrong-headedness of Macaulay's conception of Hastings' character. The authentic materials for a dispassionate examination of his wonderful administration have now been given to the world by Mr. G. W. Forrest, in his "Selections from State Papers, preserved in the Foreign Department of the Government of India, 1772–1785."

It would of course be absurd to suppose that Sheridan in his indictment of Hastings was animated by the pious, though Quixotic, zeal of Burke, or by Fox's generous, if misguided, enthusiasm for humanity. Still it would be equally unjust to assume that he regarded the Begum charge simply as an opportunity for display, or that he was not inspired by something better than a mere advocate's enthusiasm. It is true that during the pre-paration of Fox's India Bill, he had wished that it should not be made retrospective in any of its clauses, and had gone so far as to inquire of Major Scott, Hastings' champion in the House, whether, if the Governor-General were recalled, he would come home. But it is more than probable that, indolent as he naturally was, Sheridan at that date had only partially acquainted himself with the facts of Hastings' administration. Be that as it may, there can be no doubt that he seized the occasion of the Begum speech with admirable dexterity. Pitt's sudden change of front after Fox's speech on the wrongs of Cheyte Singh had practically given Hastings over to the enemy, and Sheridan spoke to an audience which was more than willing to hear him. But he made the impeachment inevitable. Unfortunately the speech was so badly reported, that it may be said to have perished. The only passage in which even a faint echo of Sheridan's eloquence is preserved, is the following description of the East India Company :—

"Alike in the political and military line could be observed auc-tioneering ambassadors and trading generals—and thus we saw a revolution brought about by affidavits ; an army employed in

executing an arrest ; a town besieged on a note of hand ; a prince
dethroned for the balance of an account. Thus they exhibited a
government, which united the mock majesty of a bloody sceptre,
and the little traffic of a merchant's counting-house, wielding a
truncheon with one hand, and picking a pocket with the other."

But if we have not the speech, we know at any rate
how it was received. He sat down not merely amidst
cheering, but amidst the loud clapping of hands, in
which the Lords below the bar and the strangers in the
gallery joined, and the excitement was so great that the
debate had to be adjourned. Such was the effect upon
the public that within four-and-twenty hours he was
offered a thousand pounds for the copyright of the speech
if he would himself correct it for the press. Possibly
from indolence, but more probably from motives of
discretion, Sheridan did not avail himself of the offer.
The opinion of highly competent judges fully endorsed
that of the public.   Burke declared it to be " the most
astonishing effort of eloquence, argument, and wit united
of which there was any record or tradition." Mr. Fox
said "all that he had ever heard, all that he had ever
read, dwindled into nothing, and vanished like vapour
before the sun." And Mr. Pitt acknowledged "that it
surpassed all the eloquence of ancient or modern times,
and possessed everything that genius or art could furnish,
to agitate or control the human mind."

The impeachment of Hastings resolved upon, Sheridan
was appointed one of the managers. So high was the
general expectation that Fox recommended him to repeat
his former speech with very little change. But Sheridan
had other views. Though there was some difficulty in

getting him to attend the committees, he had every intention of making a supreme effort, and, aided by his wife, prepared his evidence with the utmost care. When the time came, he was equal to the occasion, and for three days (June 3rd, 6th, and 10th, 1788) that audience in Westminster Hall, which Macaulay has described in an immortal passage, hung upon his lips. Fortunately we have the speech, edited by Dr. Bond, the late principal librarian of the British Museum, from the shorthand reporter's notes, almost in its entirety, and it is quite possible to form a fair idea of its merits and demerits. To look upon Sheridan as a mere rhetorician would of course be the last degree of absurdity. On the contrary, the result of a perusal of the whole speech is an impression of logical arrangement, close reasoning, and carefully selected evidence. No barrister could have marshalled the facts with a more critical sense of their legal effect; no solicitor could have got up the case with a keener eye to discrepancies in dates, or to the difference in tone between the public and private letters of Hastings and his officers. Nor were the elaborate bursts of pre-pared eloquence mere *purpurei panni;* they appear, on the contrary, to arise naturally from what has gone before, though it is true that they can be detached from the argument without materially affecting it. To attempt a summary of Sheridan's argument here would be impossible, and all that can be done is to give one or two specimens of his most finished periods, and even so we must exclude the highly-wrought description of the zenana.

Hastings claimed that he was actuated by state necessity; upon which Sheridan said :—

" My Lords, . . . I want to strip the crimes which we charge upon this man of all that false glare which, in the eyes of weak and timid men, dazzle and produce a sort of false respect to guilt.   I want to strip them of everything that can give dignity to crimes.   I want to show your Lordships the coarse and homely nature of his offences. State necessity ! No, my Lords ; that imperial tyrant, state neces- sity, is yet a generous despot.   Bold is his demeanour, rapid his decisions, and terrible his grasp.   But what he does, my Lords, he dares avow, and, avowing, scorns any other justification than the great motives that placed the iron sceptre in his hand.   But a skulking, quibbling, pilfering, prevaricating state necessity—a state necessity that tries to skulk behind the skirts of justice—a state necessity that tries to steal a pitiful justification from whispered accusations and fabricated rumours ! No, my Lords, that is no state necessity.   Tear off the mask, and you see coarse, vulgar avarice lurking behind the gaudy disguise, and adding the guilt of libelling the public honour to the fraud of private peculation."

And here are Sheridan's reflections on the desolation of Bengal occasioned by the rapacity of the Company's officers :—

" If your Lordships look over the evidence, you will see a country that, even in the time of Suja-ud-Dowla, is represented as populous— desolated.   A person looking at this shocking picture of calamity would have been inclined to ask, if he had been a stranger to what had passed in India—if we could suppose a person to have come suddenly into the country, unacquainted with any of the circum- stances that had passed since the days of Suja-ud-Dowla—he would naturally ask, ' What cruel hand has wrought this wide desolation ? What barbarian foe has invaded the country, has desolated its fields, depopulated its villages ? ' He would ask, ' What disputed succes- sion, what civil rage, what mad frenzy of the inhabitants, has induced them to act in hostility to the beneficent works of God and the beauteous works of man ? ' He would ask, ' What religious zeal or frenzy has added to the mad despair and horrors of war ? The ruin is unlike anything that appears recorded in any age.   It looks neither like the barbarities of men nor the judgment of vindictive Heaven. There is a waste of desolation, as if caused by fell destroyers never meaning to return, and who made but a short period of their rapacity. It looks as if some fabled monster had made its passage through the country, whose pestiferous breath has blasted more than its voracious appetite could devour.'

"If there had been any men in the country who had not their heart and soul so subdued by fear as to refuse to speak the truth at all upon such a subject, they would have told him that there had been no war since the time of Suja-ud-Dowla—tyrant indeed as he was, but then deeply regretted by his subjects ;—that no hostile blow of any enemy had been struck in that land; that there had been no disputed succession, no civil war, no religious frenzy; but that these were the tokens of British friendship, the marks of the embraces of British alliance—more dreadful than the blows of the bitterest enemy. That they had made a prince a slave, to make him the principal in the extortion upon his subjects. They would tell him that their rapacity increased in proportion as the means of supplying their avarice diminished. They made their sovereign pay as if they had a right to an increased price, because the labour of extortion and plunder increased. They would tell him that it was to these causes these calamities were owing. . . .

"And then I am asked to prove why these people arose in such concert. There must have been machinations, and the Begums' machinations, to produce this; there was concert. Why did they rise? Because they were people in human shape; the poor souls had human feelings. Because patience under the detested tyranny of man is rebellion to the sovereignty of God. Because allegiance to that Power that gives us the forms of men commands us to maintain the rights of men. And never yet was this truth dismissed from the human heart—never, in any time, in any age—never in any clime where rude men ever had any social feeling, or where corrupt refinement had subdued all feeling—never was this unextinguishable truth destroyed from the heart of man, placed in the core and centre of it by its Maker, that man was not made the property of man; that human power is a trust for human benefit; and that, where it is abused, revenge is justice, if not the duty of the injured. These, my Lords, are the causes why these people rose."

Here is one of Sheridan's elaborate sarcasms :—

"I beg your Lordships to observe that the committee appointed
to draw up the charges for the Commons had at that time regularly
recapitulated every one of the cruelties, the severities, and [had
dealt with] the famished state of the Khourd Mahal. Upon that
recapitulation Mr. Hastings states he had had full and perfect
explanation ; and then, having had that explanation, he makes this
concluding remark : 'Because I hold the whole series of the acts
thus connected strictly reconcilable to justice, honour, and good
policy, whoever were the parties concerned in them.' Now, my
Lords, recollect, I beseech you, the information we had from Major
Scott, the incomparable agent of Mr. Hastings, relative to this
passage. You will recollect that this incomparable Major Scott told
you at your Bar that after the defence had been finished—that after
Mr. Hastings had approved of it—Mr. Hastings added this paragraph
with his proper hand. He seems to have said to Mr. Middleton,
'You have done well indeed in owning these transactions. You
have done what I expected from you. You have acted up to that
character in your celebrated letter from Lucknow, when you offered,
God willing'—and never had a man more reason to trust in the
connivance of God for awhile to wickedness than this agent had—
'that you were ready, God willing, not only to do anything, but to
take the share of any blame upon yourself. You have done well,
my trusty agent, in this ; but you have not defended the acts—you
have not said that they were defensible by justice or policy. Give
me the paper, puny profligate ! My conscience is light ; my character
will bear it out. I will claim merit and applause from them. I will
state that they were reconcilable to honour, justice, and policy'—
by policy I presume he means that wise and just policy which con-
ducts good actions to a wise and good end. This seems the dialogue
between him and Middleton. Mr. Middleton doubtless extends the
compliment. 'I will own everything. You find character ; I'll
find memory'—and memory is his forte. 'You bear the sword ; I'll
carry the shield.' And forth these twin warriors sally to encounter
the justice and indignation of their country."

The celebrated outburst on filial piety ran as follows:—

"And yet, my Lords, how can I support the claim of filial love by argument, much less the affection of a son to a mother, where love loses its awe, and veneration is mixed with tenderness? What can I say upon such a subject? What can I do but repeat the ready truths which, with the quick impulse of the mind, must spring to the lips of every man on such a theme? Filial love—the morality, the instinct, the sacrament of nature—a duty; or, let me say, it is miscalled a duty, for it flows from the heart without effort—its delight— its indulgence, its enjoyment. It is guided not by the slow dictates of reason; it awaits not encouragement from reflection or from thought; it asks no aid of memory; it is an innate but active consciousness of having been the object of a thousand tender solicitudes; a thousand waking watchful cares, of much anxiety and patient sacrifices unremarked and unrequited by the object. It is a gratitude founded upon a conviction of obligations not remembered, but the more binding because not remembered— because conferred before the tender reason could acknowledge or the infant memory record them—a gratitude and affection which no circumstances should subdue, and which few can strengthen—a gratitude in which even injury from the object, though it may blend regret, should never breed resentment—and an affection which can be increased only by the decay of those to whom we owe it—then most fervent when the tremulous voice of age, resistless in its feebleness, inquires for the natural protectors of its cold decline."

When Sheridan, at the close of a brilliant peroration, sank as though exhausted into the arms of Burke—an excellent piece of theatrical business—it was felt by more than one critic that, rare though the display had been, it had fallen short of the speech in the House of Commons. Burke indeed exclaimed to Fox, "There, that is the true style; something between poetry and prose, and better than either." But Fox retorted with sense—"Such a mixture is for the advantage of neither, as producing poetic prose, or, still worse, prosaic poetry." Indeed, the opinion of many competent judges was that the style was too glittering and too artificial, and that with less labour a more satisfactory, if less splendid, result would have been forthcoming. Horace Walpole thought that Sheridan did not "quite satisfy the passionate expectation that had been raised, but it was impossible that he should, when people had worked themselves into an enthusiasm of offering fifty guineas for a ticket to hear him." Lord Grenville, who heard both speeches, pronounced the second vastly inferior to the first. Similarly, during the House of Common's speech, Sir Gilbert Elliot (Lord Minto) recorded that "the *bone* rose repeatedly in his throat, and tears in his eyes." But at the close of the first day's speech in Westminster Hall, he remarked, with much acuteness, that "Sheridan's flowers are produced by great pains, skill, and preparation, and are delivered in perfect order, tied up in regular though *beautiful bouquets*, and quite unlike Burke's wild and natural nosegays. I think in this respect that Sheridan's *excellence* becomes *perversely* a sort of defect; for the fine periods and passages are so *salient* from the rest, are so finished, and bear so strongly the evidence of regular and laborious composition produced by premeditation and delivered by memory, as to give the whole performance a character of design and artificial execution which keeps the author rather than his work, the orator than his speech, before you, which draws the attention away from the *purpose* to the *performance*, and which can at most exercise the wonder and admiration of his audience, leaving both their passions and their judgment unaffected."

These remarks on a particular speech may be supplemented by a criticism of a more general character, which is to be found in the "Reminiscences" of Charles Butler, the legal writer and Catholic apologist. "Sheridan," he says, "required great preparation for the display of his talents: hence he was not a debater—one who attacks and defends on every occasion that calls him forth. . . . But though Mr. Sheridan was no debater, he was sometimes most felicitous in an epigrammatic reply. He had very little information; had even little classical learning; but the powers of his mind were very great. He had a happy vein of ridicule—he could, however, rise to the serious and severe—and then his style of speaking was magnificent; but even in his happiest effusions he had too much prettiness."

Add to these qualities a commanding rather than handsome presence, a hazel eye of remarkable penetration, and a voice which, if sometimes indistinct, as on the first day of the Westminster Hall speech, was, as a rule, sonorous and rich, an utterance of extraordinary fluency, and we have Sheridan the orator before us so far as it is possible to recall him now. Of the four great speakers of the time—and it was an age of Parliamentary eloquence which will bear comparison with any that have preceded or succeeded it—Sheridan was certainly the most effective. In wit he surpassed all his contemporaries, and he avoided alike the natural redundancy of Fox, and the deliberate diffusiveness of Pitt, of whose monotonous declamation he aptly remarked, "that his was a brain that never worked but when his tongue was set agoing, like some machines that are set in motion by a pendulum." Equally true is his estimate of the permanent value of the utterances of his great rival Burke. "What will they think of the public speaking of this age in after-times when they read Mr. Burke's speeches, and are told that in his day he was not accounted either the first or the second speaker?" It is clear that Sheridan foresaw the time when Burke's philosophy would be a permanent source of political wisdom, while his own eloquence had become a voice and little more. Perhaps he did not greatly care for the opinion of posterity, and was content to win the applause of his hearers by his music, suavity, and lucidity, while Burke's harsh Irish accent, irritability, and profundity, annoyed and puzzled them. Nor can it be denied that from the practical point of view he was entirely right. Speeches are nominally made to win votes, and Sheridan is one of the very few speakers who have been able to alter materially the numbers on a division. He aimed at the ἀγώνισμα ἐς τὸ παραχρῆμα, not the κτῆμα ἐς ἀεί, and he had his reward. His methods of preparation were conducive to that end. Burke the statesman prepared his argument with care, and trusted to the inspiration of the moment for his illustrations. Sheridan the rhetorician, spent enormous labour on his ornaments, polishing his own wit, and occasionally pressing that of others into service, and having once mastered the facts, left the argument to be supplied by his innate common-sense. He treasured up his figures from similar motives.

If a good phrase could not be used in one debate, he kept it until it could be employed with effect in another. But though he had a store of prepared epigrams on hand, his impromptu sallies were fully as good as his prepared witticisms. A perusal of his great speech in Westminster Hall impresses one with the conviction that he was, like all the orators of the past century, with the exception of Burke, to be heard rather than read. If he had prepared an edition of his speeches for the press, his readers might have been tempted to venture upon the converse proposition to Fox's true paradox, and say, "They read badly, then they were good speeches." Sheridan was content that their goodness should have been established by the unanimous verdict of his contemporaries, and has considerately spared us the trouble of deciding whether his speeches read well or badly.

Of the amount of preparation which he bestowed on a great effort we have evidence in the little memoir by Professor Smyth. On May 14, 1794, Sheridan was called upon to reply to Hastings' counsel. Though he had gone over the ground before, and intended to be comparatively brief, he worked for four days and the greater part of four nights at the papers, "until the motes were coming into his eyes." The speech itself deals with minute points of evidence, and is a monument of ingenuity rather than of eloquence. It is chiefly remembered because of the practical joke played by Sheridan on his audience, in causing an elaborate search to be made for a bag full of papers which had no existence, with the evident intention of astonishing them with the readiness of his resources. But it also contains a dignified rebuke to Hastings' counsel, Mr. Plumer, who had accused Sheridan of attempting to delude a witness by handing him a wrong treaty, and, taken as a whole, forms no unworthy conclusion to Sheridan's speeches on the impeachment. As specimens of partisan oratory—and they are essentially partisan—those speeches rank among the masterpieces of human eloquence. It is a pity that they do not display some slight appreciation of the necessities of empire.

CHAPTER VII.

IF the immortals are liable to human emotions, they must groan rather than smile over the monuments raised to their memory by the "standard" biographer. And it is not easy to recall any one who has been in this respect more unfortunate than Sheridan. Not that Moore is altogether to be blamed for the inadequacy of the record that he has left us. His acquaintance with Sheridan was but slight, and dated only from the period of his decline when he was expiring—a show, indeed, though assuredly not a driveller. Nor, though he seems to have taken some pains to collect information from those who had known Sheridan in his prime, do their reminiscences seem to have been particularly valuable. Again, one can well understand that a person of Sheridan's habits would not leave behind him a very complete or carefully arranged collection of *pièces justificatives*, though it is quite possible that Moore might have examined them more carefully than he did. He seems, indeed, to have become tired of the undertaking very soon, and to have hurried over the concluding part in a perfunctory manner. Lastly, as regards Sheridan's political career, Moore wrote too soon after his death to be able to tell the whole truth about one important side of it, his relations with George IV., and was himself

8

too much of a partisan to deal fairly with many of its passages; for instance, his conduct on the outbreak of the French Revolution. In fact, if Moore had spent less time in padding out the book with windy Whig apologies, and more time in informing himself about prosaic questions like names and dates, his performance would have been far more satisfactory. Lord Melbourne, who was already in the field as Sheridan's biographer, when Moore undertook the task, is known to have expressed a regret that he yielded up his claims and materials to the professional writer.[1] Still more must posterity lament that Sheridan's accomplished grand-daughter, Mrs. Norton, never carried out her intention of giving to the world some final account of the most talented member of a talented race.

Little light is thrown on Moore's darkness by Sheridan's other biographers. Dr. Watkins' life, which appeared before Moore's, is a mere scissors and paste affair. It contains no original information, and is written from an avowedly Tory standpoint, with a considerable spice of gratuitous malice, such as the insinuation that Sheridan was not the author of "The School for Scandal." The memoir of Professor Smyth, who was tutor to his son, Tom Sheridan, deals only with the period subsequent to the death of his first wife, when Sheridan had begun to go down-hill. It contains some interesting anecdotes about his private life, and not a little malevolent gossip, for which the professor was severely taken to task by Mrs. Norton. The anonymous Octogenarian, who professed to have been brought up

[1] Mrs. Norton in *Macmillan's Magazine*, vol. iii.

at Sheridan's knee, dished up some stale anecdotes about
the Prince of Wales, and evidently, as Sheridan would
have said, "relied on his imagination for his facts," if
not "on his memory for his wit."

An attempt, then, to form an estimate of Sheridan,
apart from his writings and speeches, can at best be
extremely imperfect. The man is a riddle. At times
he was guilty of extravagances which caused superficial
observers to set him down as a brilliant butterfly
without any thought for the morrow. Nor can there
be any doubt that the vice of ostentation was one of
his most salient failings; he himself allowed he was
always in an extreme, and that he expected wings to
spring from his shoulders. Complaints of his vanity
occur again and again in Fox's letters in connection
with his political fortunes, while in society Lord John
Townshend and Fitzpatrick used to declare that he
was jealous even of a pretty woman. But the recollections of Smyth, his son's tutor, and others who knew
him intimately, enable us to pronounce, with some confidence, that deep beneath a thoughtless exterior lay a
solitary and unhappy soul. His literary tastes are an
instance in point. Spenser, not Pope as we should
imagine, was his favourite poet, while of Dryden, of
whom he was also fond, the lines most frequently on
his lips were the melancholy passage from " Palamon
and Arcite."

> " Vain men! how vanishing a bliss we crave,
> Now warm in love, now withering in the grave;
> Never, oh, never more to see the sun;
> Still dark, in a damp vault, and still alone."

Add to these indications that he was a firm believer in
dreams and portents, and had a rooted dislike of meta-
physical discussion. When his son tried to entangle
him in a debate on the doctrine of necessity, Sheridan
at once disproved its cardinal thesis, the impossibility of
indifference, by declaring that there was one thing which
he could do with total, entire, thorough indifference,
namely, listen to his questioner. He used to say, too,
that those were intolerably cruel, who, because they have
not the hopes and consolations of religion themselves,
can find in their heart to destroy them in others. If we
accept as genuine, as we surely may, these revelations
of Sheridan's inner self, it is clear that the secret of his
reckless moods may well have been a desire to silence
the promptings of a gloomy and restless imagination.
In any case, he was in many respects so great, that his
memory deserves to be treated with reverence, not, as
has been before now the case, made the subject of cheap
and obvious satire.

Towards society Sheridan's attitude was peculiar, and
in many respects unique. It sought him quite as much
as he sought it ; he ranked as the equal of the great men
of his time, and would never have accepted for a moment
the situation of a mere dependent of the nobility, afterwards occupied with much ostentation by his biographer
Moore. It is probable that he made his way through
the advocacy of the ladies, for instance, of Mrs. Crewe, to
whom he dedicated " The School for Scandal," and of
Mrs. Greville, whose accomplishments are celebrated in an
admirably turned preface to " The Critic." Mrs. Sheridan
won over the men. His devotion to so worthless a

patron as the Prince of Wales must be condemned without reserve, and, as will be noticed later on, its effect upon his own fortunes was lamentable in the extreme. But so far as we know—for the secrets of Carlton House were well kept, and it is not quite clear what were the services of a non-political nature which Sheridan rendered to the Prince beyond those of a boon-companion and amateur steward—the connection was not incompatible with a fair amount of self-respect on the part of the servant. It is true that he allowed himself to be mixed up in a dubious affair which abruptly terminated the Prince of Wales' connection with Newmarket. In 1791, Sam Chifney, the Prince's jockey, was accused of pulling Escape on the first day of the October meeting, in order to affect the betting on the next day's race, which the horse was allowed to win. Sir Charles Bunbury was thereupon sent to warn the Prince that if he continued to let Chifney ride for him no gentleman's horse would start against him, and George, in high dudgeon, broke up his stable and sedulously avoided the heath. But his conduct was not incompatible with innocence, and one does not see why Fox accused Sheridan of want of principle when he acted as the Prince's advocate before the Jockey Club.[1] Besides, with the exception of an occasional loan, he incurred no pecuniary obligations to George until towards the close of their long acquaintance. Nor was he ever servile; on the contrary, he treated appointments at Carlton House

---

[1] If, indeed, that was the occasion on which Sheridan appeared as the Prince's advocate. The information on the point is rather vague.

with the same negligence as he treated those with Smyth,
or an impecunious dramatist. Even at his worst Sheridan
seems never to have wholly lost a fine sense of the
dignity of independence.

But if Sheridan did not truckle to the leaders of
society, he took more than his share in dissipations which
they could afford and he could not. The game was
barely worth the candle. It is true that he was not a
gambler, and he made his wild bets at Brookes's, as Professor Minto has well remarked, during the period when he
was driven to extra recklessness by the death of his wife.
But his extravagant entertainments must have formed a
serious item in his embarrassments, and he persisted in
them long after his circumstances had become hopelessly
involved. Perhaps he felt that rumours of retrenchment
would only precipitate the crash. Again, his drinking
habits were notorious even in a drunken age, with serious
consequences to his character. Possibly there is not
much difference, from the standpoint of abstract morality,
between Pitt getting decorously fuddled on port, and
Sheridan becoming speechlessly "forrarder" on claret, and
latterly on brandy. But the practical bearing of their
potations on the fortunes of the two men will hardly bear
comparison. Pitt died Prime Minister, while Sheridan
died a pauper, just as the bibulous Pitt was incommoded
only by a shaking hand in private, while the convivial
Sheridan's purple face and blazing nose were the theme of
the Premier's witticisms in the House of Commons, and
the laughing-stock of many a hustings crowd. In short,
Pitt's indiscretions affected himself only, while Sheridan's
were something like a public calamity.

In spite of his over-devotion to the bottle, Sheridan's
company was the delight alike of London drawing-rooms
and of country-houses. Lord Holland tells us that
when he was in his prime nothing could exceed the
evenness of his temper, or the readiness with which he
made light of his embarrassments. He was above all
things a gentleman, urbane and full of consideration,
silent as a rule, except when he saw a chance of saying
something that was worth saying, and then he made his
effect with unerring certainty. So brilliant indeed were
his interpositions in conversation, that people used to
hint that they were prepared beforehand, and that the
attack was only delivered after a long course of elaborate
manœuvres. It may have been so in some cases, but certainly not in all, though we have little means of judging.
Boswell sets down a conversation at the Club when Sheridan was there, but he seems to have been repressed by the
presence of his elders. Fanny Burney met him at Mrs.
Cholmondeley's, in 1779, and recorded her impressions
at some length. But Sheridan's wit on this occasion confined itself to the remark that ladies should not write
verses until they were past receiving them, and his time
was chiefly spent in paying elaborate compliments to the
delighted young authoress. Again, Windham noted in
his diary that he met Sheridan at Mrs. Crewe's in 1794,
after the split in the Whig party. "The charm of his
conversation," he wrote, "and the memory of past times
made me regret the differences that now separate us."
These indications of Sheridan at his best are vague
enough, and we must be content to accept the universal verdict of Sheridan's contemporaries without

seeking to inquire into its cause. Indeed, the isolated specimens of his wit that survive are few, and quite as disappointing as those of George Selwyn, Hare, or the other brilliant talkers of the time. It was probably manner rather than matter that gave point to such a remark as— " By the silence that prevails I conclude that Lauderdale has been making a joke " ; or his reply to the same friend's request to repeat one of his stories, " I must be on my guard in future ; for a joke in your mouth is no laughing matter." Rather better was his answer to the elderly maiden lady who wished to take him for a walk in doubtful weather—" It has cleared up enough for *one* but not enough for *two* ; " and the saying that a tax upon milestones would be unconstitutional, " as they were a race that could not *meet* to remonstrate."

This much at any rate seems clear, that Sheridan's aim was to delight and amuse rather than to wound. He was a man

> " Whose humour, as gay as the fire-fly's light,
>   Played round every subject, and shone as it played,
>   Whose wit, in the combat as gentle as bright,
>   Ne'er carried a heart-stain away on its blade."

And in the same way his practical jokes in country-houses were the sheer outcome of animal spirits, and on the whole as innocent as his cricket with the children, and as harmless as his Cockney attempts at shooting. Fairly familiar specimens of them are his introduction of a young farmer to Mrs. Crewe as his friend Joseph Richardson, with the result that she was horrified at the oddness of his manners and language ; and the sermon which he wrote for Mr. O'Beirne, afterwards a bishop, and which, besides containing the unintentional blunder, "It is easier for a camel, as *Moses* says," was nothing less than a scathing comment on the penurious habits of a member of the congregation. In his later years, when past playing jokes himself, he was the inspiring spirit of Charles Mathews' most famous mystifications. Practical jokes formed indeed a prominent feature in Sheridan's more intimate friendships, as Tickell discovered when he pursued Sheridan into an ambuscade of crockery carefully prepared in a dark passage. Richardson he once compelled to pay his cab fare by beckoning him into a cab, entangling him in a violent disputation, and then jumping out with the exclamation that he would not sit any longer by the side of such a fellow. Another feature in his friendships was literary jealousy, for Sheridan was not too scrupulous in laying claim to the best part of his friends' work, and gravely assured Tierney that he had written the greater portion of Tickell's pamphlet, "Anticipation." Yet, though the relations between the two were often strained, Sheridan on the suicide of Tickell, in 1793, at once gave a home to his widow,[1] and provided for his boys, sending one of them into the Navy, and procuring for the other a situation in India, and this though he was in great straits at the time. Ten years later, when Joseph Richardson died, Sheridan arrived too late for the funeral, but characteristically made up for the neglect by persuading the clergyman to perform the ceremony over again. With these two exceptions, however, Sheridan

[1] Born Leigh. Tickell's first wife, who died in 1787, was a sister of Mrs. Sheridan.

seems to have been a man of many acquaintances rather than of many friends. Everybody knew him, but with few people did he ever open out his heart. His connection with Fox, Lord John Townshend, and Lord Lauderdale, seems to have been prompted by political motives quite as much as by the affections, and to have waned when his devotion to Carlton House caused him to act in opposition to the bulk of the Whig party. It was characterized by that love of independence which marked his relations with the Prince; he was never a parasite, and never in the habit of sponging on his associates.

Sheridan's dealings with his family were in many respects admirable. He was a good son, and though his father had treated him with harshness and caprice, his efforts to win back the old man's heart were persevering, and his attentions during his last illness unceasing. As his brother and sisters lived mostly in Ireland, Sheridan saw little of them, but their relations, thanks to the industrious correspondence of Mrs. Sheridan, seem to have been conducted on the most affectionate terms. As to his married life, the evidence is rather inconclusive. Mrs. Sheridan, beautiful, amiable, and natural, whom even the licentious Wilkes declared to be the most lovely flower that ever grew in nature's garden, seems to have been thoroughly devoted to her husband's interests. She acted as his political secretary and confidante, and watched over the interests of the theatre. There she kept an account of the receipts, read the new pieces sent in, and besides helping him in the composition of "The Duenna," is known to have adapted from the French

a spectacular piece called " Richard Cœur de Lion."
She may have been liable to be carried away by her own
and her husband's social success; but, on the whole, she
made Sheridan an excellent wife. Her letters are among
the most pleasant in Moore's book, and combine a good
deal of very excellent advice with much artless gaiety
and wholly spontaneous affection. This is how the pair
appeared to Fanny Burney in 1779 :—

"The elegance of Mrs. Sheridan's beauty is unequalled by any
that I ever saw, except Mrs. Crewe. I was pleased with her in all
respects. She is much more lively and agreeable than I had any
idea of finding her ; she was very gay and unaffected and totally
free from airs of any kind. . . . Mr. Sheridan has a fine figure,
and a good, though I don't think a handsome, face. He is tall and
very upright, and his appearance and address are at once manly
and fashionable without the smallest tincture of foppery or modish
graces. In short, I like him vastly, and think him every way
worthy of his beautiful companion. And let me tell you what I
know will give you as much pleasure as it gave me, that, by all I
could observe in the course of the evening, and we stayed very late,
they are extremely happy in each other : he evidently adores her,
and she as evidently idolizes him. The world has by no means
done him justice."

Unfortunately this mutual idolatry was by no means
incompatible with numerous quarrels. They were alike
of a romantic and jealous disposition. And while it is
certain that on Mrs. Sheridan's side there was only too
much cause for tears and recriminations, Sheridan seems
to have been racked by suspicions which had no real
foundation—notwithstanding the scandal that connected
his wife's name with that of Lord Edward Fitzgerald
—and to have been indignant that while he took his

pleasures abroad she should have entertained a circle of worshippers at home. Even in her happier moments she wrote to her sister-in-law: "So Mrs. —— is not happy; poor thing, I dare say, if the truth were known, he teases her to death. Your *very good* husbands generally contrive to make you sensible of their merit somehow or other." With all his faults as a husband, Sheridan loved her deeply, and was filled with remorse during their temporary estrangements. "Could anything bring back those first feelings?" he used to say; "Yes, perhaps, the cottage in East Burnham might." But there does not seem to have been anything like a permanent coldness; indeed the failure to appreciate so charming a companion would have argued a vulgarity of taste of which he was quite incapable. Sheridan possibly remembered a sentence in the Latin Grammar— "*Amantium iræ, amoris integratio est*"—and acted upon it. When, in spite of his constant devotion, she died of consumption in 1792, his sorrow was prolonged and violent. "The victory of the grave," he wrote, "is sharper than the sting of death;" and when shortly afterwards the infant daughter followed the mother to the tomb he was quite frantic with grief.

Of Sheridan's second marriage which, after a violent flirtation with Pamela, the adopted daughter of Mme. de Genlis, he contracted in 1795 with Miss Ogle, daughter of the Dean of Winchester, there is not much to be said except that it may be described as an exaggerated repetition of his first. He was then aged forty-four and barely able to keep his head above water. In Smyth's brief memoir of Sheridan is given an

animated picture of his restless and extravagant manner
of life immediately after the first Mrs. Sheridan's death,
of the three establishments kept up in various parts of
the country while he himself lived at an hotel, of the
livery-stables full of horses whose corn-bills were hopelessly in arrear, of a housekeeper without any money
to buy provisions, of a tutor without his salary. To
introduce order and economy into such a household
would have been a hopeless task for a young bride, and
certainly the second Mrs. Sheridan seems to have
thought that the attempt was not worth making. For,
except when provoked beyond measure by his irregularities, she seems to have been content to regard him
with an uncritical admiration, as may be judged from
her remark—"As to my husband's talents, I will not
say anything about them, but I will say that he is the
handsomest and honestest man in England."[1] Yet at
times she was severely tried. Thus Harness records
that he once discovered her walking up and down her
drawing-room in a frantic state of mind and calling her
husband a villain. After some hesitation she explained
the cause of her disorder. She had just discovered that
the love-letters written to her were copies of those which
Sheridan had sent to his first wife. Towards the other
member of the strange household, his son Tom,
Sheridan acted, as one might expect, the part of an
easy-going elder brother, rather than that of a father.
He was morbidly anxious after his health, and took
pride in his cleverness, but gave him no regular educa-

[1] Catalani, on the contrary, remarked, with much more truth, that
he had "beaucoup de talent et très peu de beauté."

tion, and, with the exception of a brief spell at soldiering, no regular profession. "Tom," he complacently remarked, "you have genius enough to get a dinner every day in the week at the first tables in London, and that is something, but that is all, you will go no farther." And when Tom said that if he went into Parliament he would attach himself to neither party, but hang out a notice, "Lodgings to let," his parent rejoined, "Yes, Unfurnished." Not a good sort of bringing-up, but much the same as Sheridan himself had received.

When Sheridan's critics talk about his want of principle, they usually mean his laxity in money matters. It was Lord Holland's theory that he had formed a totally unattainable ideal of moral rectitude, and thought nothing worth aiming at which fell short of that ideal, and that kind of reasoning is by no means rare. But Richardson, who knew Sheridan far more intimately than Lord Holland—they frequently backed one another's bills—was probably nearer the truth when he said, "that it was his sincere conviction that could some enchanter's wand touch Sheridan into the possession of fortune it would instantly convert him into a being of the nicest honour and the most unimpeachable moral excellence." And to those who possess a fluctuating income themselves, or who have friends in that position, the good sense of Richardson's observation will be at once apparent.

Sheridan's difficulties sprang from several causes. Thriftlessness was in his blood, and the tendency had been increased by his haphazard education as well as by the extraordinary rapidity of his rise. Even if he had not been naturally inclined to display, his public position both as the chief proprietor of Drury Lane and as a statesman compelled him to adopt a lavish style of entertainment. Besides, it would have been almost impossible, even if he had tried to regulate his expenditure, to anticipate with any certainty what his income from the theatre would be for the next month or even for the next week. Again, his sanguine nature induced him to underrate his embarrassments, while his habits of procrastination and want of method caused him to increase them tenfold. "Letters unanswered," groans Smyth, "promises, engagements, the most natural expectations totally disregarded. He seemed quite lawless and out of the pale of human sympathies and obligations." Certainly any one who became in any way a creditor of Sheridan's must have had many an anxious moment. Yet Smyth forgave him. So too Messrs. Hammersley, his bankers, who must have known Sheridan well, told Moore that they were certain he never meant to cheat. Again the Linleys were the victims of one of his most discreditable transactions, whereby they were induced to part with their share in Drury Lane for annuities which were never paid them. Yet the younger Linley told the same authority that he acquitted Sheridan of any low premeditated design in his various shifts and contrivances. Sheridan's tradesmen are far less deserving of sympathy, indeed it is probable that much pity has been wasted on them. His theory evidently was that it was a trial of skill between them and himself, if by repeated dunning they could get their money, well and good. But if he could talk them over or evade payment so much the

better. Boaden, in his "Life of Kemble," tells us that so
cordial were Sheridan's manners, his glance so masterly,
and his address so captivating, that tradesmen for the
most part seemed to forget that they actually wanted
money, and went away from his *levée* as if they had
only come to look at him. Their case was regarded by
him as altogether different to an obligation incurred
towards a friend. A creditor once found Sheridan in
unexpected possession of money. He was told that it was
to meet a debt of honour. The creditor thereupon burnt
his bond before Sheridan's face, and declared that he
should consider his debt as one of honour, and Sheridan
paid him at once. As a rule he was eventually driven
into a corner. Though his tradesmen had to wait for
their money, they received in the end a hundred and
fifty per cent., while as he never kept his receipts and
scorned to examine items, the dishonest were paid two or
three times over. It is clear too that a pure love of
fun was the actuating motive of many of his most ingenious subterfuges. It gave him supreme pleasure to
induce a creditor to show off the paces of a horse
while he bolted up a narrow passage, or to borrow £25
more from a lender to whom he already owed
several hundreds. "My dear fellow," he once said,
"hear reason; the sum you ask *me* for is a very considerable one; whereas I only ask you for five-and-
twenty pounds." It would be absurd to criticise
seriously a person of such an irresponsible tempera-
ment. Rogers was right when he said that in his
dealings with the world Sheridan certainly carried the
privileges of genius as far as they were ever carried by

any man. But after all posterity has no right to look upon such abuses as a matter in which it has any personal concern.

To these remarks on Sheridan's money transactions may be added, by way of illustration, some extracts from his letters to Peake, the treasurer of Drury Lane, a collection of which is among the MSS. at the British Museum. It is needless to state that they are undated. Here is one written from the Shakespeare Club on Saturday night, and couched in a curiously rambling hand :—

"You must positively come to me here and bring £60 in your pocket. Fear nothing. Be civil to all claimants, and trust me in three months there will not exist one unsatisfied claimant. Shut up the office and come here directly. Keep as punctual with Kemble as you can. . . . Borrow and fear not. . . . God bless you till I see you again, when I will make a success of all difficulties."

Here is another letter written from Newcastle where Sheridan was, as was often the case with him, "money-bound" :—

"I am so uneasy that I send Edwards back. . I am sure you will do anything possible to keep things straight for a fortnight. I am without a shilling for Tom and Mrs. S——. Try a few small loans as a personal favour to me. I never ask'd anyone but Mitchell. Don't write me a croaking letter, and you shall see what a lasting settlement I will make on my return so that you shall have no more of these anxieties. God bless you.

"I owe £40 at Newcastle."

Poor Peake ! his must have been an anxious life. At

one time he is directed to arrange some way of settling a tradesman's bill, at another to borrow money for the taxes. "Discounting small acceptance with a douceur must be the way," wrote Sheridan, and the phrase is worthy of insertion in one of his comedies. Then Mrs. Sheridan had been assured by her husband that a certain sum should be sent her every week; why did not Peake forward it? And it is needless to add that Tom Sheridan's appeals for money were incessant. The following is a specimen :—

"If you can possibly do so, send me ten or twenty pounds. I have not, by God, been master of a guinea scarcely since I have been in town and wherever I turn myself I am disgrac'd—to my Father it is in vain to apply. He is mad and so shall I be if I don't hear from you." [1]

Sheridan once told Charles Butler that his supreme ambition was to be the best possible manager of a theatre. But when a manager is compelled by his private debts to make perpetual raids on the treasury, it is evident that he falls very short of that ideal. On the other hand, it is certain that Sheridan had great and abnormal difficulties to struggle against. The nature of the ownership of theatrical property must always be a

[1] Here is another of Tom Sheridan's missives :—"To-morrow I propose setting off for Stafford town, if I can raise the supplies. I want £20 to start with, and on the road I have a hoard lying *perdue* that will carry me through. I should have wished a few minutes' conversation with you before I went. Can you give me any hint or advice as to my conduct there? Write me an answer, but, above all, do not disappoint me as to the cash. My father gives me *none*, and is mad I believe."

mystery to the layman, and Moore who might have fathomed its depths, so far as Drury Lane was concerned, seems to have shirked the difficulty with the conventional plea that it was unnecessary to bother the reader with a mass of wearisome details. As an excuse for Moore it may be stated that the variety of interests and authorities in the theatre seems to have been considerable. The profits from the private boxes did not go to the ordinary shareholders, but were under a separate and conflicting control; there were also two classes of renters, the old and the new. Besides Sheridan, so far from being the autocrat that one would imagine, was supposed latterly, at any rate, to act under the directions of a Board of Management before he accepted a piece for the stage.

"Every day's experience," he writes on May 26, 1778, after a dispute about the boxes, "with the persons I have had to deal with determines me to be trifled with in this business no longer, and paid I will be the whole of my debt some way or other. At least I will not look on and see many other persons paid before me, for no reason but because I have never pressed my claims, or because I have done the greatest service to the Property, and been the principal cause of other People getting paid at all."

Under the circumstances it can hardly be wondered that he should have been feverishly anxious to buy out as many of the other proprietors as possible, in order to get the control of the theatre into his own hands. And when once he had made up his mind, he was not a man to stick at obstacles whether they were great or small. Lacy, Dr. Ford, and the Linleys were successively got rid of; the Linleys by the ingenious expedient of annuities, but Dr. Ford demanded £17,000 in cash. It was some time before the sum was paid. Even Sheridan could not raise money by magic, and that he should have been able to do so at all argues considerable confidence on the part of his anonymous money-lenders in his business integrity and capacity.

These obligations had doubtless considerable effect upon the internal economy of the theatre. We read in Kelly's "Reminiscences" of tradesmen and scenery-painters unpaid, and it is known that the actors frequently had to go without their salaries.[1] Miss Farren once took the extreme step of absenting herself from the theatre—the occasion was during the run of Holcroft's "Force of Ridicule" in 1796—as a protest against Sheridan's conduct. But the manoeuvre does not seem to have succeeded, for after her marriage she sent her husband, Lord Derby, to press for arrears. Sheridan gently remonstrated with the noble dun, "You have taken away from us the brightest jewel in the world; and you now quarrel with us for a little dust she has left behind her." But Miss Farren's conduct seems to have been quite the exception, and the actors, an easy-going class themselves, were blind to Sheridan's faults, and full of admiration for his fertility of resource. When an alarm of fire was raised, Suett was instructed to tell the audience that if they did not keep still they would be drowned by the enormous supplies of water in the

[1] On the other hand, Reynolds the playwright declares in his "Reminiscences" that his royalties were paid with the utmost regularity. So contradictory are the statements about this perplexing man.

establishment, and to wind up his remarks by making
a face. When the King, while sitting in the royal box
in the theatre, was shot at by a madman, Sheridan was
equal to the occasion, and scribbled off an impromptu
verse to "God Save the King," which evoked from all
present a wild demonstration of patriotic fervour. Hear
Kelly, who served him in several capacities, as
manager of the Italian opera, as composer, and as an
operatic singer : "During the five-and-twenty years
through which I enjoyed his friendship and society,
I never heard him say a word that could wound the
feelings of a human being." [1] And yet Kelly in his time
was arrested for debt to an upholsterer on furniture
which Sheridan had ordered, but with which he had
been rash enough to identify himself. Never did
Sheridan's fascination of manner stand him in better
stead than when dealing with his company, and it is
only just to him to say that he never seems to have
forgotten that he was himself an actor's son. For
instance, nothing could exceed his kindness to Mrs.
Robinson, and he never took advantage of the unpro-

[1] This tribute to Sheridan does all the more credit to Kelly,
because they had more than one tiff about money-matters. Thus
there is at the British Museum the draft of a letter from Peake to
Kelly :—

"I am desired by Mr. Sheridan to express his extreme astonishment at the letter you have thought fit to write to Mr. Peake. Your
talking of 'lending *him* the £100 he *wants*,' he considers an insult
and not proceeding from ignorance, real or pretended, of the
Proposition he made you, which was that you should actually abate
£100 from your salary this year, and certify it to the Trustees, in
consequence of your having taken a sum of money last year from
the Theatre for doing so little."

tected situation in which she was placed by her scamp
of a husband.

Nor does this power of managing men exhaust the
list of Sheridan's good qualities as the director of a
theatre. He had an instinctive knowledge of the public,
and he inspired them with quite as much confidence in
his undertakings as Whitbread and the other capitalists
and business men who succeeded him. And if his own
improvidence was the cause of the numerous financial
crises that arose during his *régime*, he was unequalled in
the resource with which those crises were overcome.
Kelly tells us that he once went to Sheridan's house in
despair, the performers of the Italian Opera having
struck for arrears of salary amounting to £3,000, and
the bankers, Messrs. Morland, having declined to advance
a shilling. After two hours Sheridan appeared from his
bedroom. " Three thousand pounds, Kelly," he said
with the utmost coolness, " why there is no such sum in
nature. There is one passage in Shakespeare," he continued, " which I have always admired particularly, and
that is where Falstaff says, ' Master Robert Shallow,
I owe you a thousand pounds.'—' Yes, Sir John,' says
Shallow, ' which I beg you will let me take home with
me.' — 'That may not so easy be, Master Robert
Shallow,' replies Falstaff; and so I say unto thee Master
Mick Kelly, to get three thousand pounds may not so
easy be." However, he drove off with Kelly to the
bankers, and, continues the latter, " in less than a quarter
of an hour, to my joy and surprise, out he came, with
£3,000 in bank-notes in his hand. By what hocus-pocus
he got them, I know not, nor can I imagine even at this

moment, but those notes he brought to me, out of the
very house, where, an hour or two before, the firm had
sworn that they would not advance him another six-
pence." Similarly when the opera-house had at last to
close its doors, Sheridan allowed his co-lessee, Mrs.
Harris, to find asylum at Boulogne while he remained
and serenely faced the storm. Nor was it long before
his plausible address enabled him to dispose of the
remainder of the lease on very advantageous terms.

Even in minor matters Sheridan was probably far
more energetic than has been generally supposed.
Boaden says that although it took a Troy siege to
engage his attention, he decided at length rapidly and
correctly. In knowledge of stage-effect, as might be
expected from his life-long connection with the theatre,
he was very skilled. Kelly describes the method by
which he was directed to compose the incidental music
for " Pizarro." Sheridan, he says, made a sort of
rumbling noise with his voice, resembling a dog's gruff
bow-wow-wow, but though there was not the slightest resemblance to an air in the noise he made, yet so clear
were his ideas of effect that Kelly perfectly understood
his meaning. He seems, in fact, to have confined his
own superintendence to the production of those spectacular pieces which the low taste of the public demanded,
and where Shakespeare's plays were concerned to have
relied entirely upon Kemble. It cannot, indeed, be said
of Sheridan, that he was ambitious to raise the tone of
the stage by the production of new plays of merit. He
brought out at haphazard farces, spectacular pieces,
musical medleys, Shakespeare, and revivals of his own

comedies. But with his own exception it was an age of great actors rather than of great dramatists. Against Kemble, Mrs. Siddons, Mrs. Jordan, Miss Farren, Mrs. Powell, Bannister, and John Palmer are to be set writers like Holcroft, Cumberland, Reynolds, Monk Lewis, Mrs. Inchbald, and the other small fry whom Gifford trounced in the "Mæviad." O'Keeffe was a respectable playwright, but owing apparently to the impression that he was retained by Covent Garden, Sheridan employed him only once. Most of the plays of the younger Colman were produced at the Haymarket. And if Sheridan did not, as Kemble complained, take the trouble to look at the plays of the "great unacted," he was not the first or last manager against whom that failing has been alleged. But during the earlier years of his management the first Mrs. Sheridan performed the functions of dramatic reader, and that Sheridan himself was not altogether neglectful of rising talent is proved by several collections of unacted plays in the British Museum, in which the dialogue is freely corrected and condensed by Sheridan's hand.[1] Altogether it is probable that in spite of his

[1] Some of Sheridan's comments are perhaps worth quoting. Thus in an opera called "The Castles of Athlyn and Dunbayne," a peasant, who had appeared in the first act, is introduced very abruptly in the last. Sheridan notes that the "Peasant must be introduced or spoke of—otherwise he will be totally forgot before his entrance." In another opera without a title there is a note : "The young soldier Albert wants a horse to go three miles in search of his mistress! Make it longer." A play called "The Picturesque Incidents," after several alternative titles have been suggested, becomes, "The Artist, or Love in a Garret," and the names of some of the characters are altered, thus—Sir Gregory Greylove becomes Sir Lionel Latelove. A soliloquy by Sir Lionel with the

natural indolence and dilatoriness, he really spent much
time and trouble over the interests of the theatre, though,
no doubt, in an irregular and spasmodic manner.

It is evident that much of the chaos, that prevailed
behind the scenes during the earlier years of Sheridan's
connection with Drury Lane, was due to the incapacity of
his acting-managers. His old father, who was appointed
to the post in 1778, was not a success, owing apparently
to his fussiness. In 1782 he drifted off once more to
his "Attic Entertainments," the curious medleys of
recitations and lectures, with a facetious address to the
ladies thrown in, to which he had recourse when regular
engagements failed. Old Sherry's successor, King, was
too good-natured to do well, and his *régime* is memorable
only for the return of Mrs. Siddons to the London stage,
on which she had appeared in Garrick's time without
attracting notice. The season of 1788 opened without
a stage-manager, and it was not until October of that
year that Kemble undertook the post, and a period of
Shakesperian revivals, well - mounted and admirably
acted, began. With Kemble and Mrs. Siddons at their
best, the fortunes of Drury Lane must have been
exceedingly prosperous, and Sheridan seems to have
managed the pair with considerable tact, though Kemble

stilted opening, "It is a thousand pities that I should not have felt
sweet Love's influence sooner. Summer is gone," &c., is made by
Sheridan to begin much more naturally, "Rather late in the day to
be sure for both of us. Summer is gone." Again, a farce entitled
"Polygamy" had been sent in without the author's name. Sheridan
read it until he came to a passage where *either* of six ladies is
spoken of. "Mr. O'B's for a million" is his conclusion—possibly
O'Brien, author of "The Friend in Need."

complained that he would trouble himself very little about Shakespeare. The significant warning to Peake already quoted, " Keep as punctual with Kemble as you can," is not the only intimation of the sort that occurs in the correspondence.   Here is another:—

> " Ten Pounds will not break our bank.   Therefore by no means I beg most particularly fail to pay Kem by a draught *to-day* the order I have given him.   His wife is staying at Polesden, and after *what has happen'd there* for him to be sent back without money would be the Devil." [1]

In spite of the deference paid him, Kemble seems to have been inclined to kick against managerial proceedings, especially when he was in his cups.   Thus Boaden describes him as proclaiming in the irregular blank-verse which he affected when in that condition : " I am an *Eagle*, whose wings have been bound down by frosts and snows, but now I shake my pinions and cleave into the general air into which I was born."   But on the appearance of Sheridan he soon laid his resentment by, and a mutual reconciliation was effected by the deity to whom they were both devoted.

In 1792 a new crisis occurred in Sheridan's fortunes. The theatre, which in the previous year had been pronounced unsafe and incapable of repair, was pulled down, and pending the rebuilding the company had to find a temporary home, at considerable expense, first at the Opera House, and then at the Haymarket

---

[1] British Museum MSS.   The letter was evidently written after 1795, as Polesden was settled on the second Mrs. Sheridan as a marriage portion.

Theatre. Nor was this all; though £150,000 was easily raised for the purposes of rebuilding and paying off mortgages, the completion of the new theatre was constantly delayed, and when it was finished the architect's estimate, £75,000, was found to have been vastly under the actual cost incurred. According to Moore the new theatre started with a debt of £70,000, and though Sheridan was full of expedients, in the way of entering into new partnerships and creating new shares, it never got clear. However, though the mine of his fortunes showed signs of giving out, he laboured on with unflagging spirits.

New Drury opened on the 21st of April, 1794, with "Macbeth" performed by a cast in all probability unequalled either before or since—Kemble as Macbeth; John Palmer, Macduff; Charles Kemble, a boy of eighteen, Malcolm; Charles Bannister, Hecate; Parsons, Moody, and Baddeley, the witches; and Mrs. Siddons, Lady Macbeth. On the 2nd of July was acted, in honour of Lord Howe's victory, "The Glorious First of June," a musical trifle written to order by Cobb, from a sketch supplied him by Sheridan, and conceived, rehearsed, and produced within three days. Kelly took a part, and not having time for study, requested Sheridan that it might be short. Sheridan assured him that he would comply with his wish, and gave to the innocent Irishman the sublime and solitary speech, "There stands my Louisa's cottage; she must be either in it or out of it."

Two years later Sheridan fell a dupe to William Ireland, and was induced by him to accept the forgery,

"Vortigern," as an original play of Shakespeare's. His admirers may well wish that he had never been connected with so dubious a transaction. It is probable, however, that he looked at the matter purely from a manager's point of view, and thought that the play would win, at any rate, a success of curiosity. Besides, did not his old tutor, Doctor Parr, and the equally learned scholar, Dr. Warton, solemnly announce their belief in the genuineness of Ireland's documents? Why should Sheridan, who was not an enthusiastic admirer of the great dramatist, listen to Malone's denunciation of Ireland, or pay any attention to the grumblings of Kemble? Not that his conscience was altogether at rest. "This is strange," he said to Ireland, "for, though you are acquainted with my opinion of Shakespeare, he always wrote poetry." However his own suggestion that "Vortigern" was an immature production of the bard's came readily to his relief, and the play was produced on the 2nd of April. As is well known, the audience, after numerous expressions of restlessness, broke out into loud cries of dissatisfaction, which continued until Kemble, who had been trudging gloomily through his part, came to the line—

"And when this solemn mockery is o'er."

Then they lifted up their voices, and damned the play without mercy.

This, by the way, was not the last literary imposture with which Sheridan was concerned; but again his share in the fraud was merely that of an innocent middleman. In April, 1802, a comedy entitled "Fashionable

Friends" was produced at Drury Lane, professedly as a posthumous work by Horace Walpole. It was really by Miss Berry, and its fate was that of dismal failure.

As a welcome relief to a treasury exhausted by the Vortigern catastrophe came, in 1798, the striking success of "The Stranger," a play adapted from the German of Kotzebue by Mr. Thompson, and touched up by Sheridan. His actual share in the dialogue is not very clear, though he himself claimed, curiously enough, to have written every word of it from beginning to end. However, the familiar song, "I have a silent sorrow here," was avowedly written by him, as was its music by the Duchess of Devonshire. The literary merits of the play are nil, and its popularity was due to the wonderful acting of Mrs. Siddons as Mrs. Haller. According to an anecdote, which would appear however to lack authenticity, Sheridan did not deceive himself on the point, and sought consolation in the lines—

"The drama's laws, the drama's patrons give,
And those who live to please must please to live."

But he was too shrewd a manager not to see that the vein of German drama might be exploited with profit, and his adaptation of Kotzebue's "Spaniards in Peru," was brought out on May 24, 1799, under the title of "Pizarro." Its production was marked by his characteristic indolence. The alterations from the plot of the German original, or rather from the English translation, by some unknown hack, upon which he relied, were slight; and Kelly tells the almost incredible story that until the end of the fourth act, Mrs. Siddons, Charles

Kemble, and Barrymore, had not received their speeches for the fifth, as Sheridan was writing them upstairs in the prompter's room.[1]   Nor did he take the trouble to compose a new prologue, but reproduced that written by himself for Lady Craven's " Miniature Picture," in 1780, which had little relation to Spaniards or Peru, but contained a neat passage describing the " spark " in Hyde Park :—

> " Careless he seems, yet vigilantly sly,
> Woos the gay glance of ladies passing by,
> While his off-heel, insidiously aside,
> Provokes the caper that he seems to chide."

But he took much pains with the spectacular and musical accessories, and was feverishly anxious for the success of the piece.   It was a great though wholly spurious triumph, thanks to Kemble and Mrs. Siddons, and brought in at least £15,000 into the theatre during its first season, while the published edition sold like wild-fire.   The book was dedicated to his wife, " whose approbation of the drama, and whose peculiar delight in the applause it had received from the public, had been to *him* the highest gratification derived from its success."

Two celebrated men recorded their opinions of " Pizarro," and both were substantially just.   Charles Fox declared that it was the worst thing possible, and Pitt said that he had heard it already—in the

---

[1] Boaden, on the other hand, represents him, on the first night, as seated in a box with Richardson, and watching the performance with great anxiety.   He could hardly have been in two places at once, any more than Sir Boyle Roche.   Kelly's anecdote may be an improved edition of what occurred at one of the rehearsals.

Begum speech. The style indeed is closely akin to that of the oration, "something between poetry and prose," and one of Sheridan's additions to the dialogue, the simile of the vulture and the lamb, had actually done duty in Westminster Hall. It occurs in Rolla's address to the Peruvians :—

"Yes; they will give enlightened freedom to our minds ! who are themselves the slaves of passion, avarice, and pride. They offer us our protection; yes, such protection as vultures give to lambs—covering and devouring them ! They call on us to barter all of good we have inherited and proved, for the desperate chance of something better which they promise. Be our plain answer this —The throne we honour is the people's choice; the laws we reverence are our brave fathers' legacy ; the faith we follow teaches us to live in bonds of charity with all mankind, and die with hope of bliss beyond the grave. Tell your invaders this, and tell them too we seek no change; and, least of all, such change as they would bring us."

The whole address seems to have been composed of tags from his speeches, and particularly from one on the dangers of invasion delivered in the previous year, and it had, at any rate, the merit of being *à propos*. Indeed a madman imagined that its recitation was an invaluable specific for raising recruits for the British army, and knocked up the Prime Minister in the middle of the night to communicate the discovery to him. But there its good qualities begin and end, and Sheridan's other amplifications of the original are the merest Fitzball. The best that can be said of them is that they are few in number, and that many of the false images and "nice derangement of epitaphs," which have been ascribed to the famous dramatist, are really the contributions of the unknown hack, whose attempts to write himself up to Sheridan were about on a par with Sheridan's attempts to write himself down to his understrapper. Why the author of "The Critic" ever put his name to such a production it is easier to wonder than to guess. Perhaps at the bottom of his heart he had a sneaking fondness for "his magnificence, his noise, and his procession." He must also have felt that the piece would be more certain of success if it received his endorsement, than if it appeared as the effort—say of the humble Cobb.

Meanwhile the tide of embarrassment was beating upon the theatre with a violence which not even "Pizarro" could stem. In the year of its production an action was brought against him by some of the co-proprietors who were unable to secure their dividends. Sheridan defended in person, and won an oratorical triumph in a totally untried field. But he had to submit to comments on his improvidence from the defendants' counsel, Mr. Mansfield, which wounded him to the quick; while the Lord Chancellor, in tones of fatherly admonition, applied to him the concluding words of Johnson's "Life of Savage": "Negligence and irregularity long-continued will make knowledge useless, wit ridiculous, and genius contemptible." From time to time he made half-hearted attempts to get straight. In 1801 the following announcement appeared in *The Morning Post:*—

"The Principal Proprietor of the Theatre of Drury Lane has, at length, made an arrangement by which *Justice shall keep pace with generosity.* He retains to himself an income of £2,000 a year. To his son he allots £500. The rest of his revenue is appropriated to discharge within four years the whole of his debts."

The announcement was probably made on authority, since it is corroborated by the following letter of Tom Sheridan's to Peake, but it was never carried into effect :—

" My Father's theatrical property was of his own creating. I had no right to complain had he sold it twice over and told me to go and seek my fortune as I would (would to God I had, even my *present* standing in the army would have nearly afforded me independence), but he was not justified in day after day pointing to the Theatre as my ultimate object, and incessantly assuring me it was to be mine (as far as he could make it so), precluding me from other pursuits."

It was in vain that Sheridan called in the talents of his son to supply his own increasing deficiencies. Tom worked hard and, unlike his father, kept appointments with punctuality, while his practical and somewhat cynical knowledge of the public may be gathered from the following extract from one of his letters: " Much depends on the arrangement of the people. Remember 'St. Quentin,' and make a damnable noise and bustle whatever you do."[1] But the accession of a second Sheridan did but little to compensate the company for the loss of Kemble, who, after throwing up the stage management in 1796, and taking it up again in 1800, finally seceded altogether from Drury Lane in 1802, having failed to come to terms with Sheridan for the purchase of a quarter share in the theatre. Deprived of the great actor (who, availing himself of the fact that

[1] Dated February 13, 1809, a few days before the theatre was destroyed by fire.

"Pizarro" had been printed, transferred the attraction to Covent Garden), the management had recourse to plays like Reynolds's "Caravan," with real water, from which a still more real dog rescued a child, and to the precocious talents of the infant phenomenon, Master Betty.[1]   In those days, according to Mrs. Mathews, Sheridan was always morose, and entered the theatre as if stealthily and unwillingly. "The Circassian Bride" was announced for approaching representation when, on February 24, 1809, Sheridan was summoned from the House of Commons by the news that the theatre was on fire.   He witnessed the destruction of his property with fortitude, and perhaps with merriment.   Possibly he imagined that the catastrophe would break the run of ill-luck which had latterly haunted him.   But, if so, he was wofully mistaken.

[1] During the run of "The Caravan," Dignum said to Sheridan, "There is no guarding against illness, but really——"—"Really what?"—"I am so unwell that I cannot act any longer than to-night."—"You! my good fellow," was the rejoinder, "you terrified me; I thought you were going to say that the dog was taken ill." Another version of the story transfers the compliment to Reynolds.

CHAPTER VIII.

SHERIDAN'S great speech in Westminster Hall, in 1787, forms a fairly definite landmark in his political life. Up to that point in his career he had acted, on the whole, as a consistent member of the Whig party, animated perhaps by no very deep convictions, but still zealously faithful to his friends and admirably disinterested in his conduct. Sheridan remained incorruptible to the last. But already he had formed that connection with the Prince of Wales which induced him to separate his interests from those of his associates, and eventually led to his isolation and extinction. The fate that overtook him was just—

> "The heart whose hopes could make it
> Trust one so false, so low,
> Deserved that thou should'st break it."

But it is evident that his aims were not altogether ignoble, though his action in their pursuit was occasionally the reverse of satisfactory. Naturally a man of vast confidence in his own powers, he hoped to make himself indispensable to the Prince, partly through the charms of his conversation and the attractiveness of

his conviviality, but chiefly through the wisdom of his
advice in political emergencies.   Then when the King:
died or became incapable of conducting the affairs of
the nation, he would naturally step into the place of the
chief confidential adviser of the head of the State.   A.
great ambition truly for a political adventurer to enter-
tain, but unfortunately founded on several miscalcula-
tions.   In the first place, George III. defied probability
by continuing to hold the reins of power until long after
his son had ceased to identify his fortunes with the Whig
friends of his youth.   Secondly, the Prince was quite
clever enough to make use of Sheridan without being
governed by him.   As a rule George had recourse to his
advice in the first instance, but Burke or Sir Gilbert
Elliot were frequently called in when a political or semi-
political apology had to be penned, while on the floor of
the House of Commons Fox and Grey, who had influence as well as abilities, were commissioned to act as
his champions rather than Sheridan.   In fact, after the
manner of princes, he played off one adherent against
the other, committing to Sheridan, who had most at stake,
the -execution of the most thankless tasks.   Sheridan
never became more than a subordinate, a minor actor on
the ignoble stage of Carlton House politics.   Seldom
has a prince been more faithfully served, and seldom has
a servant been treated with greater ingratitude.

Though Sheridan had acted for several years in a
private capacity as the lay keeper of the Prince's apology
for a conscience, the first occasion on which he came
prominently forward as his confidential friend was in
1787.   The circumstances, so far as Sheridan was con-

cerned, were briefly these : In April of that year the
Prince's debts were, not for the first time, brought before
the notice of Parliament, and Mr. Rolle incidentally
raised the question of the Prince's alleged marriage with
Mrs. Fitzherbert. A lie came naturally to George, and
he promptly authorized Fox to contradict Rolle's statement, a request with which Fox, unsuspecting in disposition and not too nice in morals, promptly complied. A
revulsion of feeling naturally ensued, and the House
voted the increase of allowance, but then the Prince had
to reckon with Mrs. Fitzherbert, who was naturally much
distressed. He had recourse in the first instance to Mr.
Grey, but that high-minded statesman would give him no
help. "Well, then, Sheridan must say something," was
the Prince's significant determination, and to Sheridan
accordingly fell the unworthy lot of paying a few vapid
compliments to Mrs. Fitzherbert, in which the whole
question was begged, and the royal lie indirectly con-
firmed. After Sheridan was dead, George added the
finishing touch to his baseness by authorizing Croker to
deny that the speech had been made on his authority;
it was, he declared, actuated solely by the tears of Mrs.
Fitzherbert.

Unwarned by experience, Sheridan, on the illness of
the King in the following year, plunged again into the
mazes of princely intrigue. In the absence of Fox in
Italy, he directed the scramble for power, and, with a
keen eye for want of character, opened a secret negotia-
tion with Thurlow, the Lord Chancellor. On his return
from abroad, the step was condemned by Fox, who had
a deserved contempt for Thurlow, and had more than

half promised the Chancellorship to Lord Loughborough
in the event of a change of government; still for the
moment it promised well.   For himself Sheridan was
content to bide his time, and accepted the inferior post
of Treasurer of the Navy *in posse*.   In fact, with the
arrival of Fox, the conduct of affairs passed from
Sheridan's hands, but it cannot be said that what
influence he possessed was exercised, during the debates
on the Regency Bill, on the side of discretion.   On the
contrary, when Fox committed himself to the assertion.
of the Prince's unalienable right to assume the government, Sheridan, though the damaging effect of the theory
upon the fortunes of the Opposition was immediately
perceived, set himself to pour oil on the flames.   A few
days later, while asserting the right of the Prince of
Wales to an unrestricted regency, he reminded the
House of "the danger of provoking that Prince to assert
his right."   "It was such a blunder," wrote Grenville
to his brother, "that I never knew any man of the
meanest talents guilty of before.   During the whole time
that I have sat in Parliament I have never seen such an
uproar as was raised by his threatening."   Pitt immediately availed himself of such rash tactics.   Sheridan's
language was characterized as "an indecent menace
thrown out to awe and influence the proceedings of the
House."   "To assert the inherent right of the Prince
of Wales to assume the government," he declared later
on, "is virtually to revive those exploded ideas of the
divine and indefeasible right of princes which have so
justly sunk into contempt and almost oblivion."   The
Prime Minister was winning all along the line, when the

recovery of the King, under the care of Dr. Willis, consummated his triumph.

The rout of the Opposition left many bitter memories behind it, particularly in the minds of the two men who had been most confident of victory — Sheridan and Burke. It is true that their quarrel was almost inevitable. Fortune had marked them out as rivals, and the rivalry was deepened by the vastness of their ambitions, the jealousy of their characters, and the insecurity of their positions. But it is from this period that the antagonism became markedly exhibited, and the Prince of Wales was its conscious or unconscious fomenter. To Burke he allotted the composition of a vindication of his conduct in the shape of a letter to Mr. Pitt, to Sheridan the task of criticising it, and Burke never forgave the interference. These latent differences among the members of Fox's staff became of vital importance on the outbreak of the French Revolution. It was clear from the outset which side Burke would take. His love of liberty was tempered with a due respect for authority, and he deplored alike the rapid advances of the French towards democracy, and the tumultuous means by which those advances were effected. Fox, on the contrary, espoused the cause of the revolution with a genuine, if unreasoning, enthusiasm, and it was clear that, with its leaders thus divided, the dissolution of the Whig party was imminent. The first passage of arms between Burke and Fox, however, which occurred in 1790, during a debate on the army estimates, would have passed off without result had not Sheridan intervened with a speech which, uncompromising though it was, no doubt was unnecessarily treated by Burke as a declaration of war between the last speaker and himself. "Henceforth," he declared, "his honourable friend and he were separated in politics," and though efforts were made to reconcile the two, the rupture was never healed. As a natural sequel came, in the following session, the familiar and dramatic separation between Burke and Fox, and in 1793 the secession of a considerable portion of the Whig party, including three-fourths of its aristocratic chiefs, to the ministerial benches.

Sheridan was of course not entirely responsible for the turn affairs had taken. Still he had given the first blow to the wedge that had split old political friendships asunder, and he now set himself by his sarcasms to foil all attempts at reconciliation. At the expense of Burke he committed himself, in the course of 1793, to the unworthy sneer, "It is hard that he whom we have drummed out of the regiment as a deserter should be lurking within our lines as a spy." The accusation was unjust, though Burke's theatrical exclamation, "I quit the camp!" certainly provoked a retort. Nor was there any real justice, though there was some plausibility, in his famous condemnation of the seceding Whigs who had accepted office and honours from Pitt, "Let them go and hide their heads in their coronets." In short, his mind during this period seems to have been wholly out of gear, partly perhaps from private and domestic reasons, but partly also from consternation at the completeness of his own handiwork of ruin. Neither in his criticisms on the progress of the Revolution, nor in his comments upon the war which was now forced upon

England, is there much wisdom or patriotism to be
found. It is unnecessary, therefore, to dwell upon
them at any length. But if Sheridan was infected by
faction he was at least superior to treachery. It is more
than probable that both then and afterwards he could
have made his peace with the Government, but in spite
of his pecuniary difficulties he remained faithful to his
principles. All credit to him for his incorruptibility.

"Sir," he once said in the hearing of Byron, "it is easy for my
Lord G——, or Marquis B——, or Lord H——, with thousands
upon thousands a year, some of it either *presently* derived or *inherited*
in sinecure or acquisitions from the public money, to boast of their
patriotism and keep aloof from temptation; but they do not know
from what temptation those have kept aloof, who had equal pride,
at least equal talents, and not unequal passions, and, nevertheless,
knew not in the course of their lives what it was to have a shilling
of their own."

Sheridan appears to have been rather drunk when he
made the observation, but he never spoke a truer word.
Whatever his private conduct may have been, his
political record will bear the minutest scrutiny.

The mutiny at the Nore in 1797 gave Sheridan an
opportunity of setting himself right with the majority
of his fellow-countrymen. On that occasion he acted
a truly worthy part, and by his strenuous advocacy of
prompt measures for its suppression, undoubtedly
checked something like a national panic. We know
also from Lord Holland's "Memoirs of the Whig
Party," that he opposed the ill-judged secession of the
Opposition from Parliament which had taken place a
few weeks previously, and though he shared in the

movement for awhile, soon returned to the House of
Commons, and resumed a fairly active part in debate.
In the absence of his leader he appears to have considered that he was entitled to take up a line of his
own, and his conciliatory attitude towards the ministry
was vehemently resented at St. Ann's Hill. Thus in
1797 Fox commented on the "incurable itch which
Sheridan seemed to have of distinguishing his conduct
from that of those with whom he wishes to be supposed
united;" and in 1802 he wrote to Grey, "whether
Sheridan will be with us I do not *know*, and I suspect
you do not *care*, or even that your wishes would be that
he should not." Stories were current that he had
separated from Fox; some went even so far as to assert
that his services had been solicited by the Crown, but to
both statements he gave the most complete and vehement
denial.

The simple fact seems to be—even if due allowance
is made for Sheridan's love of popularity, which was
considerable—that having learnt wisdom by experience,
he repented the tone adopted by himself and other
extreme Whigs at the outbreak of the revolutionary war.
At last he began to see that unless something like a
national effort was made, the decline and fall of the
British Empire was imminent.

"If," said he, in the year 1800, "we are threatened to be
deprived of that which is the charter of our existence, which has
procured for us the commerce of the world, and been the means of
spreading our glory over every land—if the rights and honours of
our flag are to be called in question, every risk should be run and
every danger braved. Then we should have a legitimate cause of

war—then the heart of every Briton would burn with indignation, and his hand be stretched forth in defence of his country. If our flag is to be insulted, let us nail it to the top-mast of the nation; there let it fly while we shed the last drop of our blood in protecting it, and let it be degraded only when the nation itself is overwhelmed."

Such being the general aspect of affairs, the formation of the Addington Ministry in 1801 seemed to Sheridan to give an opening for a fusion of parties. It was obvious that the administration only existed on the sufferance of Pitt, and that to prevent Pitt from returning to office the Whig Opposition must either support the Government, or form a coalition with the "new Opposition," headed by Lord Grenville. As the Grenvilles formed an ultra war-party, the former step was the more logical of the two, and Sheridan accordingly adopted an ironically favourable tone towards "the Doctor" in public. Thus in a debate on the army estimates, after characterizing the dislike entertained by the Opposition towards the Minister as unreasonable, and quoting against them, amidst shouts of laughter, the familiar lines—

> "I do not like thee, *Doctor* Fell,
> The reason why I cannot tell," &c.,

he proceeded to urge that the foreign policy of the Government had been all that could be desired. Addington, he said, had been a great success as Speaker;

"but did the House expect that when he was minister he was to stand up and call Europe to order? Was he to send Mr. Coleman, the Sergeant-at-Arms, to the Baltic, and summon the Northern Powers to the Bar of the House? Was he to see the Powers of Germany scrambling like members over the Benches, and say—Gentlemen must take their places? Was he to cast his eye on the Tuscan Gallery and exclaim that strangers must withdraw? Was he to stand across the Rhine, and say, The Germans to the right and the French to the left? If he could have done these things, he (Sheridan), for one, should always vote that the Speaker of the House should be appointed the Minister of the country. But the Right Honourable Gentleman had done all that a reasonable man could expect him to do."

Meanwhile he took care to assure Addington, in private, that his support was entirely disinterested. "My visits to you," he said, "may possibly be mis-construed by my friends, but I hope you know, Mr. Addington, that I have an unpurchaseable mind." And to prove that this was not mere talk he declined for his son the appointment of Registrar of the Vice-Admiralty Court at Malta, and possibly refused office for himself.

Sheridan, however, soon saw that if he went over to Addington he must go over alone, unaccompanied even by the small band of the friends of the Prince of Wales. For the Prince, influenced by the refusal of the Government to accept the offer of his military services, declined to give them any active support; and Fox, who looked upon Addington as a "vile fellow," had, in spite of loud murmurs from his followers, determined on joining the Grenvilles. For the moment Sheridan was absolutely isolated. Windham taunted him with behaving like a new recruit; no sooner had he fallen into the Government ranks than he fired off his musket, without waiting for the word of command.

Cobbett addressed to him ten scathing letters, in which
the apostasy of the " Political Proteus " was denounced
in uncompromising terms. Accordingly he had to make
his peace with his party. " He is," wrote Fox to Grey, on
April 6, 1804, " very desirous of getting right again, but
you will easily believe my dependence on him is not
very firm." To prove his sincerity he turned and rent
Addington, upon whose appearance in Windsor uniform
to announce the declaration of war with France he
passed the happy comment, " The Right Honourable
Gentleman has assumed his favourite character of the
sheep in wolf's clothing." And he was one of the most
assiduous of the assailants of the dying Pitt. There,
however, he met his match, and in their last encounter
the Treasury Bench scored an easy victory. The
Prime Minister satirized Sheridan's eloquence as " an
explosion of froth and air, of all his hoarded repartees,
all his matured jests, the full contents of his common-
place book ; " and Gillray drove the application home
by his famous cartoon, " Uncorking old Sherry."

In spite of his rejuvenated Whiggery, Sheridan was
condemned for the remainder of his life to wander
without the fold. Though it is not true, as has been
asserted, that he was excluded during the last illness of
Mr. Fox, he never regained the confidence of that
usually placable heart. By Grey he had long been
disliked, while the cold and haughty Grenville resented
his efforts to prevent the coalition. On the formation of
the Ministry of all the Talents, Sheridan was excluded
from the Cabinet, and compelled to put up with the
office of Treasurer of the Navy, for which he was

notoriously unfit. The reason assigned for the slight
was that his convivial habits rendered him an unsafe
possessor of Cabinet secrets, which, said Sheridan, might
have been a valid objection if there were any secrets to
be disclosed. After the death of Fox, Sheridan wished
to succeed him as the representative of Westminster—
indeed he had long coveted the honour, and is even said
by Lord Holland to have advised Fox's retirement from
public life in the year 1800, with the insidious design of
stepping into his shoes as the representative of that
popular constituency. On this occasion, however, Lord
Grenville interposed, and Sheridan was compelled to
withdraw his candidature in favour of that of Lord
Percy, though he was returned at the general election
about three weeks later. He revenged himself by de-
clining to attend Lord Grenville's meetings, and by
ridiculing his downfall in 1807, owing to the injudicious
revival of the Catholic question. "I have often," he
said, "heard of people knocking their brains against a
wall, but I never before knew of any one building a wall
expressly for the purpose."

From this time forward, Sheridan, though still affecting to keep up the Whig connection, adopted Carlton
House politics, pure and simple. After the death of
Fox, the Prince of Wales declined to pose any longer as
a party man, while his factotum disliked alike Grenville,
Grey, and Whitbread, who had become a leader of the
Opposition. Sheridan was a good hater, and when, in
1810, the Prince, now become Regent, showed a disposition to summon the Whig chiefs to form a Government, he had no hesitation in tripping up their heels.

The reply which Grenville and Grey, at the request of the Regent, had drawn up in answer to the addresses of the two Houses, was subjected by Sheridan to a searching criticism, which even Moore, partizan as he was, is constrained to confess that it thoroughly deserved; and a totally different form of answer, drawn up by the Prince and himself, was adopted. The remonstrance of Grenville only evoked from Sheridan ridicule and satirical rhymes, and the Tories in consequence remained in power. In the following year when the negotiations were renewed, Sheridan suppressed in his communication to Lord Grenville all intimation that the Household were ready to resign, and over this supposed obstacle the attempt to form a government broke down. His conduct was not too scrupulous, but he was a broken and disappointed man with a long series of slights to avenge.

This was Sheridan's last action of importance in the theatre of politics. In the month of September following he stood once more for Stafford, but his Westminster candidature, added to his known impecuniosity, had alienated the electors, and he was defeated. And so his long political career closed in failure. Throughout it had been entirely characteristic of him. His name is unconnected with a single legislative measure. No real conviction is to be traced in his casual advocacy of the causes of reform and abolition; his praises of the French Revolution are inspired quite as much by faction and party spirit as by any real zeal for liberty. Though proud of being an Irishman, he showed little appreciation of the wants of Ireland; and his criticism

of Pitt's free-trade proposals, and of the act of union
with England, was equally unsound. During his later
years the friendship of the Prince of Wales hung like
a loadstone about his neck, and in combination with his
inordinate vanity induced him to attempt the *rôle* of a
moderator between parties, with the result that he was
alienated from his friends, and gained in return only the
empty compliments of his enemies. Yet it may fearlessly be asserted of him that he was a patriot at heart,
and his support of Pitt and Addington, even if its
motives were partly personal, was a more worthy course
of action than Fox's petulant retirement to St. Ann's
Hill. Above all, he was entirely incorrupt. In spite of
his necessities no offers of place or pension could tempt
him to go over to the enemy, and with the exception of
three brief intervals of office he began, continued, and
ended in Opposition. He may have been an adventurer,
and he was doubtless an insubordinate follower. But
though he fought for his own hand as the *enfant perdu*
of politics, he was not a mere condottiere whose sword
was at the service of the highest bidder. Besides to a
man of wit, party shibboleths are apt in the end to
become rather ridiculous, and genius may fairly revolt
against the edicts of grandees of the stamp of Portland
or Grenville, to which it is the duty of mediocrity to
submit. After detraction has said its worst about
Sheridan, his remains a great name in the annals of the
House of Commons.

CHAPTER IX.

SEVERAL years before he ceased to be a member of Parliament, Sheridan had become a hopelessly ruined man. The destruction of Drury Lane Theatre in 1809 had deprived him of his only permanent source of income, with the exception of his salary as Receiver of the Duchy of Cornwall—an appointment to which he was presented by the Prince of Wales in 1804—and that was in all probability anticipated. It is true that he still retained a considerable portion of the property, but the committee which was formed for the rebuilding of the theatre, with Whitbread as its guiding spirit, declined to allow him any connection with the new undertaking. They were willing to buy him out for £28,000, but out of that sum the Linleys and others were to be paid, and the satisfaction of their claims could not have left a large balance at the bankers. Further, Sheridan himself, evidently wishing to get the blind side of the committee, proposed the concession that his claims should not be satisfied until after the theatre was built. His mortification when he was held to his word was extreme, and his correspondence with Whitbread is a painful exhibition of the contest between wounded pride and pressing necessity.

✝ The explanation of the mystery of Sheridan's existence during the last years of his life is that the sum total of his debts was nothing like so large as was generally imagined. When his pecuniary affairs were examined in 1808 it was found that his *bonâ-fide* obligations were only about ten thousand pounds. Indeed, had it not been for the false pride which forbade him to contest any of his creditor's claims, however extravagant, his friends might possibly have extricated him from his difficulties, though those difficulties would always have been liable to recur. He preferred rather to pay his duns in proportion to the importunity and extravagance of their demands. How he contrived to rub along may be gathered partly from the draft of an agreement among the Sheridan MSS. in the British Museum, by which he made over the copyright of his dramatic works to James Grant Raymond for £600,[1] and partly from Mr. Clayden's "Life of Samuel Rogers," where it appears that the poet-banker helped him to raise money on Mrs. Sheridan's farms about Leatherhead. It would be remembered too that Sheridan's powers of fascination were undoubtedly great, even at this period of his life, and he relied upon them as a weapon of defence. Kindhearted tradesmen were easily persuaded to postpone presenting their accounts; and he was even competent in an emergency, as Byron records with wondering admiration, to soften the heart of an attorney. "Would you have us proceed against Old Sherry?" asked the

---

[1] The arrangement appears to have fallen through, but he must have been in great straits to think of parting with the copyright for so small a sum.

legal adviser of Sheridan's wine merchant—whose bill, one would think, must have been a heavy one.— " Besides what would be the use of it." And Byron records that the attorney was so completely talked over by Sheridan, that had his client come in, honest man though he was, with all the law and some justice on his side, he would promptly have been thrown out of the window. ✗

Mr. Whitbread seems, indeed, to have been almost the only person, with whom Sheridan had business dealings, whose determination he did not at one time or another disarm. That cool-headed man however was inexorable, and it was to his refusal to advance £2,000 out of the sum due to Sheridan by the Drury Lane Committee for his share in the property, that he attributed his failure at Stafford. That defeat was closely followed by a breach between Sheridan and the patron for whom he had sacrificed his political career. Nor can it be denied that the Regent's version of the story, as given to the world for the first time in the Croker Papers, is greatly to Sheridan's discredit. It appears that though he refused, as stated by Moore, to re-enter Parliament as a direct nominee of the Regent, he did not scruple to borrow £3,000 pounds from him, to purchase a seat at Wootton Bassett, on his own account.[1] The distinction drawn shows a curious obliquity of moral vision, but it may even be doubted

[1] The Regent was not the most trustworthy of men, but in this instance he seems to have been speaking the truth. His version of the story, as given in the Croker Papers, is corroborated by information given by Lord Holland to Moore on the authority of Sheridan himself.

whether Sheridan ever had any real intention of devoting the money to the purpose for which it was ostensibly procured. He made no attempt to visit the borough, the money was lodged in the hands of a solicitor by Sheridan without the slightest intimation that it had been advanced to him with any restrictions, and it was promptly devoted to the payment of certain pressing debts, among them one to the solicitor. The fraud was of course discovered, and Sheridan's explanation, by which the solicitor was made to blame, must be pronounced ingenious rather than convincing. "I never," continued the Regent, in tones of edifying if over-elaborated morality, "saw Sheridan (to speak to) after; not that it was much worse in principle than other things of his, nor that I had given orders to exclude him, but it was felt by Sheridan himself to be so gross a violation of confidence—such a want of respect, and such a series of lies and fraud, that he did not venture to approach me, and, in fact, he never came near me again." And yet a really royal heart would have overlooked the injury, in consideration of Sheridan's lifelong devotion.

His exile from Carlton House must have been felt bitterly by the old courtier. Yet he fought bravely against his troubles, and in the society of Moore, Rogers, and Byron, his wit still sparkled, even though as Byron recorded, "It was always saturnine and sometimes savage; he never laughed—at least that *I* saw, and I watched him." "I have seen him," Byron states in another place, "cut up Whitbread, quiz Madame de Staël, annihilate Colman, and do little less by some others (whose names, as friends, I set not down) of good

fame on their side."[1] The cutting up of Whitbread must
have been a most congenial occupation to Sheridan, and
of his recorded sayings few are neater than his comment
on the brewer-politician's allusion to the Phœnix in his
address for the opening of Drury Lane. "But Whitbread made more of this bird than any of them—he
entered into particulars, and described its wings, beak,
tail, &c. ; in short, it was a *Poulterer's* description of
a Phœnix." What other sarcasms Sheridan may have
uttered at the expense of the new theatre we do not
know. But this we do know, that when, three years
after it was built, he was induced by Lord Essex to see
Kean, he promptly made his way to the green-room,
where a bumper to his health was drunk by the assembled
actors. And so the father of the stage bade farewell to
the old region of his glory.[2]

[1] Mrs. Mathews, on the other hand, declares that "Mr. Colman
fairly broke him down with the force of his vivacity." However,
Byron could appreciate Sheridan, while Mrs. Mathews evidently
writes about him with prejudice.

[2] Readers of Moore will remember how Whitbread offered Mrs.
Sheridan a box at the new theatre, and how she annoyed that pre-
cise person by not sending him an answer. It appears from the
MSS. at the British Museum that she did at last reply, though not
until more than three months after Whitbread's first letter, and
probably without Sheridan's knowledge.

"MY DEAR MR. WHITBREAD,—I beg you will return my best
thanks to the Committee for the attention they have shewn me
respecting a Box at Drury Lane Theatre. I know nothing of the
same kind that could have been equally valuable to me, and I
accept the offer in the terms in which it is made.

"With much gratitude, I am,
"My dear Mr. Whitbread,
"Affectionately yours,
"Sept. 14, 1812.   E. T. SHERIDAN."

On the whole, however, Sheridan's decadence must
have been a most melancholy spectacle, even though in
his cups he was still capable of so supreme a witticism as
his solemn assurance to the watchman, who came upon
him "fuddled, bewildered, almost insensible," that his
name was Wilberforce. Byron was right when he
urged—

> " But should there be to whom the fatal blight,
> Of failing wisdom yields a base delight,
> Men who exult when minds of heavenly tone,
> Jar in the music which was born their own.
> Still let them pause—Ah ! little do they know
> That what to them seemed Vice might be but Woe.
> Hard is his fate on whom the public gaze
> Is fix'd for ever to detract or praise ;
> Repose denies her requiem to his name,
> And Folly loves the martyrdom of fame. "

That martyrdom was destined to be terribly acute. The
sum arising from the sale of his theatrical property in
1813-14 was soon exhausted by the various claims upon
it, and, his immunity from arrest having ceased with his
disappearance from the House of Commons, he made
the acquaintance of the interior of the sponging-house,
" to the profanation," as he characteristically termed it,
" of his person." All his most cherished possessions
were disposed of one after the other, including the
famous portrait of his first wife, as St. Cecilia, by the
hand of Sir Joshua. Here is a statement which he seems
to have drawn up about this time for his friend Peter
Moore, and it shows the way that his money went :—

				£	s.	d.
Paid Bill	...	...	...	50	0	0
Interest, 2¼ years	...	...	...	6	5	0
Attorney's Bill...	...	...	...	9	4	6
Expenses of arrest	...	...	...	2	6	0
				£67	15	6 [1]

And yet, low as he had fallen, he retained much elevation of feeling. If society shut its gates against him, he never whined outside, and Moore records that he rarely borrowed money from the obscure friends who stood by him to the last. It is only as we read the concluding chapters of Moore's biography that we realize the full force of Richardson's estimate of his friend's character.

When his last illness came upon him Sheridan was practically deserted by all, except that small band of men who are remembered solely for their charity to the dying genius, Peter Moore, Ironmonger, and "Hat" Vaughan. Tom Sheridan was abroad, and already a victim to that hereditary consumption under which he sank not many years after his father's death. Mrs. Sheridan had borne with her husband's failings patiently, as he would have been the first to acknowledge, but she too was afflicted by a fatal disease. The Regent declared, on the authority of Vaughan, that during Sheridan's last days upon earth she was too ill to leave her own bed. But Smyth certainly saw her when he came to inquire after his old patron, and it may be that the gruesome description of their common misery given in the Croker Papers

[1] British Museum MSS.

owes a good deal to the Regent's imagination, which was notoriously exuberant. It certainly is not a pleasant picture.

✗

"They had hardly a servant left. Mrs. Sheridan's maid she was about to send away, but they could not collect a guinea or two to pay the woman her wages. When Vaughan entered the house he found all the reception rooms bare, and the whole house in a state of filth and stench that was quite intolerable. Sheridan himself he found in a truckle bed in a garret, with a coarse blue and red coverlid, such as one sees used as horse-cloths, over him; out of this bed he had not moved for a week, . . . and in this state the unhappy man had been allowed to wallow, nor could Vaughan discover that any one had taken any notice of him, except one old female friend—whose name I hardly know whether I am authorised to mention—Lady Bessborough, who sent £20."

Even as Sheridan lay dying, and possibly starving, his creditors pressed upon him; and had it not been for the prompt assistance of Rogers, and the stout interposition of his doctor, he would have been carried off to die in the sponging-house. When it was too late some efforts were made to assist him in his necessity. Indeed, it is only just to point out that until an eloquent appeal for succour was inserted in *The Morning Post* many of his old friends may well have been in ignorance of his actual condition. But it was all the same to Sheridan whether they were heartless or simply thoughtless, and the Regent was justified in characterizing the ice and currant water that was sent from Holland House as "an odd contribution." From the Regent himself came £200, which Mrs. Sheridan, so soon as the danger of actual want had passed away, returned. The smallness of the sum is naturally visited by Moore, on the evidence before him, with just condemnation. But it seems that the Regent, who naturally remembered his last money transaction with Sheridan, was really in ignorance of the position in which his old servant was placed ; that he set no limit to the sum to be advanced; and that Mr. Vaughan, who was himself in ignorance that Sheridan was destitute of the necessities of life, only consented with reluctance to accept the £200. Besides, the gift was made anonymously. In fact, taking into consideration the circumstances as a whole, the candid critic will probably pronounce that so far from being to the Regent's discredit, the gift constitutes one of the few really worthy actions with which his name is connected in the page of history.

The anguish of his last hours thus in a measure relieved, Sheridan met death bravely and wittily. "My friends," he said, "have been very kind in calling upon me, and in offering their services in their respective ways ; Dick W—— has just been here with his *will-making* face." To his old friend Lady Bessborough he sent a last message that his eyes would look up to the coffin-lid as brightly as ever. He passed beyond the clutch of the sheriff's officer on July 7, 1816, and a few days later came a magnificent funeral in Westminster Abbey to heighten the contrasts in his tragic close.

> " How proud they can press to the funeral array,
>   Of him whom they shunn'd in his sickness and sorrow !
> How bailiffs may seize his last blanket to-day,
>   Whose pall shall be held up by nobles to-morrow !

Was this then the fate of this high-gifted man,
The pride of the palace, the bower, and the hall—
The orator, dramatist, minstrel—who ran
Through each mood of the lyre, and was master of all?"

THE END.

INDEX.

—◆—

BIBLIOGRAPHY.

BY

JOHN P. ANDERSON

(British Museum).

I. WORKS.

The Works of the late Right Honourable Richard Brinsley Sheridan. 2 vols. London, 1821, 8vo.

The Works of the late Right Honourable Richard Brinsley Sheridan. Collected by Thomas Moore, Esq. A new edition. Complete in one volume. Leipsic, 1833, 8vo.

The Works of the Right Honourable Richard Brinsley Sheridan, with a memoir by James P. Browne, M.D. Containing extracts from the life by Thomas Moore. 2 vols. London, 1873, 8vo.

Also issued the same year, in one volume, without "The Camp, a musical entertainment," not written by Sheridan, but included in the two-volume edition.

The Works of Richard Brinsley Sheridan. Dramas, poems, translations, speeches, and unfinished sketches. Edited by F. Stainforth. London, 1874, 8vo.

II. DRAMATIC WORKS.

The Dramatic Works of Richard Brinsley Sheridan, containing

The School for Scandal, The Rivals, The Duenna, The Critic. London [1795 ?], 12mo.

The Dramatic Works of Richard Brinsley Sheridan. With some observations upon his personal and literary character. Greenock, 1828, 12mo.

The Dramatic Works of Richard Brinsley Sheridan. With a biographical and critical sketch. By Leigh Hunt. London, 1840, 8vo.

——Another edition. London, 1846, 8vo.

The Dramatic Works of Richard Brinsley Sheridan. With a memoir of his life, by G. G. S[igmund]. London, 1848, 8vo.
> Part of "Bohn's Standard Library."

The Dramatic Works of Richard Brinsley Sheridan, with a biographical and critical sketch Edited by Ludwig Gantter. Stuttgart, 1854, 8vo.
> No. 3 of "The Standard Poets of Great Britain."

The Plays of Richard Brinsley Sheridan, with an introduction by Henry Morley. London, 1883, 8vo.
> Part of *Morley's Universal Library.*

Sheridan's Comedies. The Rivals and the School for Scandal. Edited, with an introduction, and notes to each play, and a biographical sketch of Sheridan, by Brander Matthews. Illustrations by E. A. Abbey, etc. Boston, 1885, 8vo.

Dramatic Works of Sheridan and Goldsmith. With Goldsmith's Poems. 2 vols. London, 1884, 32mo.

——Another edition. London [1886], 16mo.
> Part of "Cassell's Miniature Library of the Poets."

The Rivals, and the School for Scandal. London, 1886, 16mo.
> Forms part of "Cassell's National Library."

The Dramatic Works of Richard Brinsley Sheridan. London [1887], 8vo.
> Forms part of "Cassell's Red Library."

Plays of Sheridan. Containing The Rivals, The School for Scandal, The Critic. London, 1889, 8vo.
> Part of "Bohn's Select Library."

The Rivals, The School for Scandal, and other plays of Richard Brinsley Sheridan. London, 1890, 8vo.

III. SPEECHES.

Speeches of the late Right Honourable Richard Brinsley Sheridan. (Several corrected by himself.) Edited by a Constitutional Friend. 5 vols. London, 1816, 8vo.

The Speeches of the Right Honourable Richard Brinsley Sheridan. (*Modern Orator*, vol. 1.) London, 1845, 8vo.

The legislative independence of Ireland vindicated in a speech of Mr. Sheridan's on the Irish Propositions in the British House of Commons, etc. Dublin, 1785, 8vo.

Speeches in the Trial of Warren Hastings. Edited by E. A. Bond. 4 vols. London, 1859-61, 8vo.
> Vols. 1 and 4 contain Sheridan's Speeches, taken from Gurney's reports.

The Speech of R. B. Sheridan in bringing forward the fourth charge against Warren Hastings relative to the Begums of Oude.

The second edition. London, 1787, 8vo.

Speech before the High Court of Parliament on summing up the evidence on the Begum Charge against Warren Hastings, Esq. London, 1788, 8vo.

Speech in the House of Commons, on the 21st of April, 1798, on the motion to address His Majesty, on the present alarming state of affairs. [London ? 1798] 8vo.

Speech of Richard Brinsley Sheridan in the House of Commons in reply to Mr. Pitt's speech on the Union with Ireland. Dublin, 1799, 8vo.

The Speech of Richard Brinsley Sheridan, in the House of Commons (8th December 1802), on the motion for the Army Establishment for the ensuing year. London, 1802, 8vo.

——New edition. London, 1803, 8vo.

——The Speech of R. B. Sheridan in the House of Commons, Dec. 8, 1802, on the Army Estimates, etc. Birmingham [1802], 8vo.

IV. SELECTIONS.

The Beauties of Sheridan, consisting of selections from his poems, dramas, and speeches, by A. Howard. London [1834 ?], 12mo.

V. SINGLE WORKS.

The Camp, a Musical Entertainment. By Richard Brinsley Sheridan [or rather by R. Tickell]. London, 1795, 12mo

The Camp, a Musical Entertainment. Another edition. London, 1803, 12mo.

——Another edition. (*Cumberland's British Theatre*, vol. 32.) London [1829], 12mo.

Clio's Protest; or, the Picture Varnished [signed Asmodeo— *i.e.*, R. B. Sheridan]. (*The Rival Beauties*, etc., pp. 5-17.) London [1771], 4to.

——Clio's Protest; or, "The Picture" varnished, with other poems. London, 1819, 8vo.

A Comparative Statement of the two Bills for the better government of the British possessions in India, brought into Parliament by Mr. Fox and Mr. Pitt; with explanatory observations. London, 1788, 4to.

——Third edition. London, 1788, 4to.

Crazy Tales. By the late Richard Brinsley Sheridan [or rather by J. H. Stevenson. In verse]. London, 1815, 12mo.

The Critic; or, a tragedy rehearsed. A dramatic piece in three acts. London, 1781, 8vo. Produced at Drury Lane in 1779.

——Fourth edition. London, 1781, 8vo. The title-page is engraved.

——Another edition. Dublin, 1785, 12mo.

——Another edition. (*Cawthorn's Minor British Theatre*, vol. 6.) London, 1807, 8vo.

——Another edition. (*Modern British Drama*, vol. 5, pp. 642-659.) London, 1811, 8vo.

——Another edition. (*The London Theatre, by Thomas Dibdin*, vol. 8.) London, 1814, 16mo.

——Another edition. (Mrs. Inchbald's *Collection of Farces*, vol. 3.) London, 1815, 12mo.

The Critic. Another edition.
London, 1820, 8vo.
    Oxberry's *New English Drama*,
    vol. 9.
——Another edition. (*The Lon-
don Stage*, vol. 1.) London
[1824], 8vo.
——Another edition. (*British
Drama*, vol. 1, pp. 554-566.)
London, 1824, 8vo.
——Another edition. (*Cumber-
land's British Theatre*, vol. 15.)
London [1829], 12mo.
——Another edition. (*Penny
National Library*, vol. 5.)
London [1830], 8vo.
——Another edition. (*The Acting
Drama*, pp. 27-38.) London,
1834, 8vo.
——Another edition. (*Lacy's
Acting Edition of Plays*, vol.
8.) London [1850], 12mo.
——Another edition. (*British
Drama*, vol. 3, pp. 657-670.)
London, 1865, 8vo.
The Duenna: a Comic Opera.
London, 1775, 8vo.
    Produced at Covent Garden on
    the 21st November, 1775.
——The Duenna; or, the Double
Elopement; a comic opera as it
is acted at the Theatre, Smoke
Alley, Dublin. [Dublin] 1786,
8vo.
——Another edition. London,
1794, 8vo.
——Another edition. Dublin,
1794, 12mo.
——Another edition. (*Mrs.
Inchbald's British Theatre*, vol.
19.) London, 1808, 12mo.
——Another edition. London,
1818, 8vo.
    Oxberry's *New English Drama*,
    vol. 2.
——Another edition. (*London
Stage*, vol. 1.) London [1824],
8vo.
——Another edition. (*Duncombe's*

Edition, vol. 39.) London
[1825], 12mo.
——Another edition. (*British
Drama*, vol. 2, pp. 1102-
1119.) London, 1826, 8vo.
——Another edition. (*Cumber-
land's British Theatre*, vol. 2.)
London, 1829, 12mo.
——Another edition. (*The Penny
National Library*, vol. 5.) Lon-
don [1830], 8vo.
——Another edition. (*The Lon-
don Theatre*, pp. 78-95.) Lon-
don, 1834, 8vo.
——Another edition. (*British
Drama*, vol. 4, pp. 1055-1072.)
London, 1865, 8vo.
——Songs, duets, trios, etc.,
in the Duenna, etc. Sixth
edition. London, 1775, 8vo.
——Eighth edition. London,
1776, 8vo.
——Fifteenth edition. London,
1776, 4to.
——Twenty-fifth edition. London, 1778, 8vo.
——Twenty-ninth edition. London, 1783, 8vo.
The Forty Thieves; a romantic
drama, by R. B. Sheridan and
Colman the Younger. (*Duncombe's Edition*, vol. 2.) London [1825], 8vo.
The General Fast; a lyric ode:
with a form of prayer proper
for the occasion; and a dedica-
tion to the King. By the
author of the Duenna. London
[1775 ?], 4to.
The Love Epistles of Aristænetus,
translated from the Greek into
English metre [by N. B.
Halhed and R. B. Sheridan];
with notes. London, 1771,
8vo.
——Second edition, corrected.
London, 1773, 8vo.

The Love Epistles of Aristænetus. Translated by R. B. Sheridan and Mr. Halhed. (*Erotica. The Elegies of Propertius*, etc.) London, 1854, 8vo.
The Love Epistles comprise pp. 430-496. A re-issue of this work appeared in 1883.

An Ode to Scandal ; to which are added, Stanzas on Fire. Second edition. London, 1819, 8vo.

Pizarro, a tragedy in five acts, taken from the German drama of Kotzebue, and adapted to the English stage, by R. B. Sheridan. London, 1799, 8vo.

——Twentieth edition. London, 1799, 8vo.

——Twenty-sixth edition. London, 1800, 8vo.

——Another edition. (*London Stage*, vol. 1.) London [1824], 8vo.

——Another edition. London, 1824, 8vo.
Oxberry's *New English Drama*, vol. 20.

——Another edition. (*British Drama*, vol. 2, pp. 982-1000.) London, 1826, 8vo.

——Another edition. (*Cumberland's British Theatre*, vol. 1.) London, 1829, 12mo.

——Another edition. (*The Penny National Library*, vol. 5.) London [1830], 8vo.

——Another edition. (*The Acting Drama*, pp. 95-111.) London, 1834, 8vo.

——Another edition. (*Lacy's Acting Edition of Plays*, vol. 27.) London [1856], 12mo.

——Another edition, with historical notes, by Charles Kean. London [1856], 8vo.

——Another edition. (*British Drama*, vol. 1, pp. 65-81.) London, 1864, 8vo.

The Rivals, a Comedy, as it is acted at the Theatre Royal in Covent Garden. London, 1775, 8vo.
Produced at Covent Garden on the 17th of January 1775.

——Second edition. London, 1775, 8vo.

——Third edition. London, 1776, 8vo.

——Another edition. (*Collection of New Plays*, vol. 4, pp. 143-282.) Altenburgh, 1778, 8vo.

——Fifth edition. London, 1791, 8vo.

——Another edition. Dublin, 1793, 12mo.

——Another edition. (*Mrs. Inchbald's British Theatre*, vol. 19.) London, 1808, 12mo.

——Another edition. (*Modern British Drama*, vol. 4, pp. 619-648.) London, 1811, 8vo.

—— Another edition. (*The London Theatre, by Thomas Dibdin*, vol. 1.) London, 1815, 16mo.

——Another edition. London, 1818, 8vo.
Oxberry's *New English Drama*, vol. 1.

——Oxberry's Edition. London, 1820, 12mo.

——Another edition. (*British Drama*, vol. 1, pp. 346-368.) London, 1824, 8vo.

——Another edition. (*The London Stage*, vol. 1.) London [1824], 8vo.

——Another edition. (*Cumberland's British Theatre*, vol. 2.) London, 1829, 12mo.

—— Another edition. (*The Penny National Library*, vol. 5.) London [1830], 8vo.

——Another edition. (*Sinnett's Family Drama*, pp. 1-80.) Hamburg, 1834, 8vo.

The Rivals. Another edition. (*The Acting Drama*, pp. 39-60.) London, 1834, 8vo.
——Another edition. (*Duncombe's Edition*, vol. 40.) London [1852], 12mo.
——Another edition. (*Lacy's Acting Edition of Plays*, vol. 83.) London [1858], 12mo.
——Truchy's edition. Paris, 1861, 8vo.
——Another edition. (*Library of English Literature*, No. 1.) Gouda [1885], 8vo.
——The Rivals. Illustrated by F. M. Gregory. London [1890], 4to.
    Only 100 copies printed.
St. Patrick's Day. (*Cumberland's British Theatre*, vol. 28.) London [1829], 12mo.
    Produced at Covent Garden in 1775.
——Another edition. (*Lacy's Acting Edition of Plays*, vol. 114.) London [1879], 12mo.
The School for Scandal, a Comedy. Dublin [1777 ?], 8vo.
    Performed on the 8th of May 1777.
——Another edition. Dublin, 1781, 12mo.
——Fourth edition. Dublin, 1782, 12mo.
——Another edition. The real and genuine School for Scandal. London, 1783, 12mo.
——Another edition. (*A volume of plays, as performed at the Theatre Royal, Smoke Alley, Dublin.*) [Dublin], 1785, 16mo.
——Another edition. Dublin, 1787, 12mo.
——Fifth edition. London, 1788, 12mo.
——Another edition. (*Collection of English Plays*, vol. 1.) Copenhagen, 1807, 12mo.

The School for Scandal. Another edition. London, 1823, 8vo.
——Another edition. (*The London Stage*, vol. 4.) London [1824], 8vo.
——(Duncombe's edition, vol. 1.) London [1825], 12mo.
——Another edition. (*British Drama*, vol. 2, pp. 1600-1624.) London, 1826, 8vo.
——Another edition. (*Cumberland's British Theatre*, vol. 14.) London [1829], 12mo.
——Another edition. (*The Penny National Library*, vol. 5.) London [1830], 8vo.
——Another edition. (*The Acting Drama*, pp. 1-26.) London, 1834, 8vo.
——Another edition. (Sinnett's *Family Drama*, pp. 147-226.) Hamburg, 1834, 8vo.
——Another edition. London [1837], 8vo.
    Part of vol. vii. of Webster's "Acting National Drama."
——Another edition. Paris, 1852, 12mo.
——Another edition. (*Lacy's Acting Edition of Plays*, vol. 27.) London [1856], 12mo.
——Another edition. Leipzig, 1861, 8vo.
——Another edition. Göttingen, 1863, 8vo.
——Another edition. (*British Drama*, vol. 2, pp. 385-410.) London, 1864, 8vo.
A Trip to Scarborough, a Comedy . . . altered from Vanbrugh's Relapse; or, Virtue in Danger, etc. London, 1781, 8vo.
    Produced at Drury Lane, 24th February, 1777.
——Another edition. (Mrs. Inchbald's *Modern Theatre*, vol. 7.) London, 1811, 12mo.
——Another edition. (*The Lon-*

don Theatre, by Thomas Dibdin, vol. 14.) London, 1815, 16mo.
——Another edition. London, 1824, 8vo.
   Oxberry's *New English Drama*, vol. 20.
——Another edition. (*London Stage*, vol. 2.) London [1824], 8vo.
——Another edition. (*Cumberland's British Theatre*, vol. 4.) London, 1829, 12mo.
——Another edition. (*The Penny National Library*, vol. 5.) London [1830], 8vo.
——Another edition. (*The Acting Drama*, pp. 61-77.) London, 1834, 8vo.
——Another edition. (*Lacy's Acting Edition of Plays*, vol. 103.) London [1875], 12mo.
Verses to the memory of Garrick. Spoken as a monody, at the Theatre Royal in Drury Lane. London, 1779, 4to.
——Second edition. London, 1779, 4to.
——Another edition. The Tears of Genius. A monody on the death of Mr. Garrick. Dublin, 1780, 12mo.

VI. APPENDIX.

BIOGRAPHY, CRITICISM, ETC.

Albion, *pseud.*—Second edition. Four pleasant epistles written for the entertainment and gratification of four unpleasant characters—viz., A very exalted subject in his Majesty's Dominions [George Prince of Wales]. The most unpatriotic man alive [C. J. Fox]. The most artful man alive [R. B. Sheridan], and second childhood [E. Burke]. London, 1789, 4to.

Bardsley, Samuel A.—Critical remarks on Pizarro, a tragedy taken from the German drama of Kotzebue, and adapted to the English stage by R. B. Sheridan, etc. London, 1800, 8vo.

Britton, J.—Sheridan and Kotzebue. The enterprising adventures of Pizarro . . . with biographical sketches of Sheridan and Kotzebue, etc. London, 1799, 8vo.

Brougham, Henry, *Lord.*—Historical Sketches of Statesmen who flourished in the time of George III. London, 1839, 8vo.
   Mr. Sheridan, pp. 210-218.

Byron, Lord.—Monody on the death of the Right Honourable R. B. Sheridan, written at the request of a friend, to be spoken at Drury Lane Theatre. [By Lord Byron. London, 1816, 8vo.

Cobbett, William.—The Political Proteus. A view of the public character and conduct of R. B. Sheridan, Esq., etc. London, 1804, 8vo.

Encyclopædia Britannica.—Encyclopædia Britannica. Eighth edition. Edinburgh, 1860, 4to.
   Richard Brinsley Sheridan, by James Browne, LL.D., vol. xx., pp. 106-112.
——Ninth edition. London, 1886, 4to.
   Richard Brinsley Sheridan, by Professor W. Minto, vol. xxi., pp. 797-800.

Fitzgerald, Percy.—The Lives of the Sheridans. 2 vols. London, 1886, 8vo.

Fry, Alfred A.—A Lecture on the Right Honourable R. Brinsley Sheridan, delivered at Constantinople. Constantinople, 1862, 8vo.

Gent, Thomas.—Monody : to the memory of the Right Honourable Richard Brinsley Sheridan. London, 1816, 4to.

Georgian Era.— The Georgian Era : Memoirs of the most eminent persons, who have flourished in Great Britain, from the accession of George the First to the demise of George the Fourth. London, 1832, 12mo.
Richard Brinsley Sheridan, vol. 1, pp. 364-376.

Harsha, David A.— The most eminent Orators and Statesmen of ancient and modern times. Philadelphia [1875], 8vo.
Richard Brinsley Sheridan, pp. 240-255.

Hazlitt, William.—Lectures on the English Comic Writers. London, 1819, 8vo.
Sheridan, pp. 334-388.

Heron, D. C.—Richard Brinsley Sheridan. (*Afternoon Lectures on Literature and Art, Dublin,* 1867 *and* 1868.) Dublin, 1869, 8vo.

Lefanu, Alicia.—Memoirs of the life and writings of Mrs. Francis Sheridan, with remarks upon a late life of the Right Honourable R. B. Sheridan, etc. London, 1824, 8vo.

Mangin, Edward.—A Letter to Thomas Moore, Esq., on the subject of Sheridan's "School for Scandal." Bath, 1826, 8vo.

Mathias, T. J. — The Political Dramatist of the House of Commons in 1795. A satire [in verse by T. J. Mathias]. London, 1796, 8vo.

Molloy, J. Fitzgerald. — Famous Plays, etc.
Sheridan's Rivals, and School for Scandal, pp. 175-218.

Moore, Thomas.—Memoirs of the life of the Right Honourable Richard Brinsley Sheridan. London, 1825, 4to.

Nicoll, Henry James. — Great Orators. Burke, Fox, Sheridan, Pitt. Edinburgh, 1880, 8vo.

Oliphant, Margaret Oliphant.— Sheridan. London, 1883, 8vo.
Part of the *English Men of Letters* Series.

Pepperpod, Peter, *pseud.* — The Literary Bazaar . . . with a pic-nic elegy on Richard Brinsley Sheridan. London, 1816, 8vo.

Philips, Charles.—A Garland for the grave of Richard Brinsley Sheridan. London, 1816, 8vo.

Rae, W. F.—Wilkes, Sheridan, Fox, etc. London, 1874, 8vo.
Richard Brinsley Sheridan, pp. 141-245.

S., R. B.— The Critick Anticipated ; or, the Humours of the Green Room ; a farce [written in imitation of Sheridan's piece]. London, 1779, 8vo.

Satiricon, Barnley, *pseud.*—More Kotzebue ! The origin of My own Pizarro, a farce. [A satire on Sheridan's "Pizarro."] London, 1799, 8vo.

Scott, John.—Observations upon Mr. Sheridan's Pamphlet intituled "Comparative Statement of the two Bills for the better government of the British Possessions in India." London, 1788, 4to.

—Second edition. London, 1788, 4to.

—Third edition. London, 1789, 4to.

Sheridan, Richard Brinsley.—The case of the Stage in Ireland, wherein the conduct and abilities of Mr. Sheridan are examined, etc. Dublin [1758], 8vo.

—— La Governante ; or the Duenna ; a new comic opera. The poetry by Mr. Badini, the music by Signor Bertoni. London, 1779, 8vo.

——The struggles of Sheridan, or the Ministry in full cry. [A satire in verse.] London, 1790, 4to.

——Memoir of the life of R. B. Sheridan, with a concise critique upon the New Tragedy of Pizarro. London, 1799, 8vo.

——A Critique on the Tragedy of Pizarro, as represented at Drury Lane Theatre with such uncommon applause. To which is added, a new prologue, that has not yet been spoken. London, 1799, 8vo.

——Mr. Fox's title to Patriot and Man of the People disputed ; and the political conduct of Mr. Sheridan and his adherents accurately scrutinised, etc. London, 1806, 8vo.

——An Address to Richard Brinsley Sheridan, on the public and private proceedings during the late election for Westminster, etc. London, 1807, 8vo.

——Authentic Memoirs of the life and death of R. B. Sheridan. With an estimate of his character and talents. London, 1816, 8vo.

——Lines on the death of —— [i.e., R. B. Sheridan]. London, 1816, 8vo.

——Lines supposed to be written on the death of the late R. B. Sheridan, Esq. . . . [Edited] with additional lines, Addressed to Friendship [by M. Cancanen]. London [1816], s.sh. folio.

The Life of R. B. Sheridan, with the remarks of Pitt, Fox, and Burke on his most celebrated speeches. Second edition. London [1816 ?], 8vo.

——Sheridaniana ; or, Anecdotes of the life of Richard Brinsley Sheridan ; his table-talk, and bon-mots. London, 1826, 8vo.

——Sheridan and his Times ; by an Octogenarian who stood by his knee in youth, and sat at his table in manhood. 2 vols. London, 1859, 8vo.

Smyth, William.—Memoir of Mr. Sheridan. Leeds, 1840, 8vo.

Stewart, C. B.—A Second Letter to Mr. Sheridan. With strictures on the general conduct of opposition. By a Suffolk Freeholder [C. B. Stewart]. Bury St. Edmunds, 1796, 8vo.

Surface, Joseph, *pseud.* — An epistle from Joseph Surface, Esq., to Richard Brinsley Sheridan, etc. [A satire.] London, 1780, 4to.

Watkins, John.—Memoirs of the public and private life of the Right Honorable Richard Brinsley Sheridan, with a particular account of his family and connexions. London, 1817, 4to.

Weiss, Kurt.—Richard Brinsley Sheridan, als Lustspieldichter. Leipzig, 1888, 8vo.

Wharton, Grace and Philip, *pseud.* *i.e.*, Mrs. Katharine and J. C. Thomson.—The Wits and Beaux of Society. 2 vols. London [1860], 8vo.
  Richard Brinsley Sheridan, vol. ii., pp. 97-161.

Whipple, Edwin P.—Essays and Reviews. 2 vols. Third edition. Boston, 1856, 8vo.
  Richard Brinsley Sheridan, pp. 250-302.

Zinck, A. G. L.—Congreve, Vanbrugh og Sheridan. Kjøbenhavn, 1869, 8vo.

MAGAZINE ARTICLES.

Sheridan, Richard Brinsley. Monthly Review, vol. 89, 1819, pp. 225-235 ; same article, Analectic Magazine, vol. 14, 1819, pp. 341-350. — Blackwood's Magazine, vol. 20, 1826, pp. 25-41, 201-214. — North American Review, vol. 4, 1826, pp. 32-38.—Dublin University Magazine, vol. 9, 1837, pp. 469-485, 600-615, 672-695; same article, Eclectic Magazine, vol. 36, pp. 656-672. — Southern Literary Messenger, vol. 3, 1837, pp. 470-472. — Fraser's Magazine, vol. 26, 1842, pp. 103-111.—North American Review, by E. P. Whipple, vol. 66, 1848, pp. 72-110.—Universal Review, vol. 3, 1860, pp. 75-98 ; same article, Littell's Living Age, vol. 64, pp. 771-785.—Fortnightly Review, by W. F. Rae, vol. 8, 1867, pp. 310-332; same article, Littell's Living Age, vol. 95, pp. 102-115. — New Monthly Magazine, vol. 148, 1871, pp. 705-715. — Gentleman's Magazine, by H. B. Baker, vol. 243, 1878, pp. 304-320. — Temple Bar, vol. 60, 1880, pp. 488-503 ; same article, Littell's Living Age, vol. 148, pp. 131-140.—Nation, by A. V. Dicey, vol. 39, 1884, pp. 136, 137.

——and his Biographers. Macmillan's Magazine, by the Hon. Mrs. Norton, vol. 3, 1861, pp. 178-179.—Princeton Review, by B. Matthews, vol. 18 N.S., 1884, pp. 292-303.

Sheridan, Richard Brinsley.

——and his Wives. Gentleman's Magazine, by Percy Fitzgerald, vol. 260, 1886, pp. 42-61.

——as an Orator. Hogg's Instructor, by G. Gilfillan, vol. 1 N.S., 1853, pp. 361-370.

——at Work. Chambers's Journal, vol. 47, pp. 193-198.

——The Critic. Tinsley's Magazine, by C. Matthews, vol. 11, 1872, pp. 414-418. — Lippincott's Magazine, by J. B. Matthews, vol. 24, 1879, pp. 629-635.

——Duels with Captain Mathews. All the Year Round, vol. 18, 1867, pp. 128-136.

——The Duenna. Harper's New Monthly Magazine, by J. B. Matthews, vol. 60, 1880, pp. 501-508.

——Faulkland. New Monthly Magazine, by F. Jacox, vol. 132, 1864, pp. 414-421.

——Life of. Portfolio, vol. 3, 4th Series, 1817, pp. 365-377.

——Life and Writings of. Dublin University Magazine, by J. W. Calcraft, vol. 46, 1855, pp. 38-55.

——Loves of. Belgravia, by Percy Fitzgerald, vol. 14, 1871, pp. 163-175.

——Mrs. Oliphant's Life of. Academy, by T. H. Caine, vol. 24, 1883, pp. 171, 172.—Month, vol. 49, 1883, pp. 281-286.—Athenæum, Aug. 25, 1883, pp. 234-236.—Literary World (Boston), vol. 15, 1884, pp. 22, 23.—Spectator, Jan. 26, 1884, pp. 124, 125.—Saturday Review, vol. 56, 1883, pp. 379, 380.

——Moore's Life of. Edinburgh Review, by F. Jeffrey, vol. 45, 1826, pp. 1-48.—Blackwood's

Sheridan, Richard Brinsley.

Edinburgh Magazine, vol. 19, 1826, pp. 113-130, 351-353.—United States Literary Gazette, vol. 3, 1826, pp. 361-367.—Monthly Review, vol. 108 N.S., 1825, pp. 149-162.—Quarterly Review, by J. W. Croker, vol. 33, 1826, pp. 561-593.—Bentley's Miscellany, vol. 1, 1837, pp. 419-427.—New Monthly Magazine, vol. 14 N.S., 1825, pp. 474-484.—Christian Observer, vol. 26, 1826, pp. 478-494.—Boston Monthly Magazine, vol. 1, 1826, pp. 438-445.—Metropolitan Quarterly Magazine, vol. 1, 1836, pp. 203-255.—Portfolio, vol. 20 N.S., 1825, pp. 401-413.——*Richard Grant White on.* Atlantic Monthly, Oct. 1883, pp. 566-570.

Sheridan, Richard Brinsley.

——*Rivals.* Scribner's Monthly, by J. B. Matthews, vol. 21, 1880, pp. 183-189.—— ——*First Cast of Rivals.* Theatre, by Austin Brereton, June 2, 1884, pp. 281-289.—— ——*Rivals and School for Scandal.*—All the year Round, July 24, 1886, pp. 541-547.——*School for Scandal.* Appleton's Journal, vol. 2 N.S., 1877, pp. 556-562.—London Magazine, vol. 5, 1822, pp. 481-483.—Academy, by F. Wedmore, vol. 21, 1882, pp. 109, 110.—Theatre, by Percy Fitzgerald, March 1, 1882, pp. 171-174.——*Sheridaniana.* London Magazine, vol. 5 N.S., 1826, pp. 97-103.

VII. CHRONOLOGICAL LIST OF WORKS.

THE WALTER SCOTT PRESS, NEWCASTLE-ON-TYNE.

THE CANTERBURY POETS.

EDITED BY WILLIAM SHARP.

A NEW COMPREHENSIVE EDITION OF THE POETS.

Square 12mo, Uncut, 40 cents; Limp Mor., $1.75; Padded Grained Mor., $2.00; Padded Polished Mor., $2.00; Half Mor., $1.50. Also Sets of above, 2 vols. in paper box, cloth, gilt, the Set, $1.00. Also in cloth, gilt stamp and edges, 75 cents per volume.

PRESS NOTICES OF RECENT VOLUMES.

The Lady of Lyons, and other Plays. By Lord Lytton, with an Introduction by Farquharson Sharp.

"Mr. Sharp's essay is able. As for Lytton's dramas, the poetic merits of two of them are indisputable, while the *Lady of Lyons* is probably, taking it all round, the best acting play written in this country during the last sixty years; and many people will be glad to have the text of all three pieces in the neat and handy form in which they are here presented."—*Scottish Leader.*

Selections from the Greek Anthology. Translations by Dr. Richard Garnett, Andrew Lang, Goldwin Smith, etc. Edited by Graham R. Tomson.

"Both in selection and arrangement Mrs. Tomson has displayed the utmost taste. . . . The introduction is exactly what it should be. It conveys a great deal of information, yet is sympathetic and picturesque from beginning to end."—*Scots Observer.*

PETER SIMPLE.	By Captain Marryat.
PAUL CLIFFORD.	By Bulwer Lytton.
EUGENE ARAM.	By Bulwer Lytton.
ERNEST MALTRAVERS.	By Bulwer Lytton.
ALICE; OR, THE MYSTERIES.	By Bulwer Lytton.
RIENZI.	By Bulwer Lytton.
PELHAM.	By Bulwer Lytton.
LAST DAYS OF POMPEII.	By Bulwer Lytton.
THE SCOTTISH CHIEFS.	By Jane Porter.
WILSON'S TALES OF THE BORDERS.	
THE INHERITANCE.	By Miss Ferrier.
ETHEL LINTON.	By E. A. W.
A MOUNTAIN DAISY.	By Emily Grace Harding.
HAZEL; or, Perilpoint Lighthouse.	By Emily Grace Harding.
CHARLES O'MALLEY.	By Charles Lever.
MIDSHIPMAN EASY.	By Captain Marryat.
BRIDE OF LAMMERMOOR.	Sir Walter Scott.
HEART OF MIDLOTHIAN.	Sir Walter Scott.
LAST OF THE BARONS.	By Bulwer Lytton.
OLD MORTALITY.	By Sir Walter Scott.
TOM CRINGLE'S LOG.	By Michael Scott.
CRUISE OF THE MIDGE.	By Michael Scott.
COLLEEN BAWN.	By Gerald Griffin.
VALENTINE VOX.	By Henry Cockton.
NIGHT AND MORNING.	By Bulwer Lytton.
MANSFIELD PARK.	By Jane Austen.
LAST OF THE MOHICANS.	By Fenimore Cooper.
POOR JACK.	By Captain Marryat.
JANE EYRE.	By Charlotte Brontë.
DOMBEY AND SON.	By Charles Dickens.
VANITY FAIR.	By W. M. Thackeray.

WILSON'S TALES OF THE BORDERS

AND OF SCOTLAND.

HISTORICAL, TRADITIONARY, AND IMAGINATIVE.

Revised by ALEXANDER LEIGHTON.

A complete storehouse of fact and romance of the Border Wars between England and Scotland. No collection of tales published in serial form ever enjoyed so great a popularity as the "Tales of the Borders."

In 24 vols., sold separately, price 40 cents per vol., or $9.60 the set.
Also in 12 volumes, sold only in sets, price $10.00.

NEW PRESENTATION VOLUMES.

The "Windsor Series" of Poetical Anthologies

Printed on Antique Paper. 12mo.

Cloth, $1.50; Half Blue Polished Mor., gilt, $2.75; Half Mor., gilt, $3.00; Half Calf, gilt, $3.00; Padded Grained Mor., $3.75.

WOMEN'S VOICES. Edited by Mrs. William Sharp.
SONNETS OF THIS CENTURY. Edited by William Sharp.
CHILDREN OF THE POETS. Edited by Prof. E. S. Robertson.
SACRED SONG. Selected by Samuel Waddington.
A CENTURY OF AUSTRALIAN SONG.
Selected and Edited by Douglas B. W. Sladen, B.A., Oxon.
JACOBITE SONGS AND BALLADS. Edited by G. S. Macquoid.
IRISH MINSTRELSY. Edited by H. Halliday Sparling.
THE SONNETS OF EUROPE. Selected by S. Waddington.
EARLY ENGLISH AND SCOTTISH POETRY.
Selected and Edited by H. Macaulay Fitzgibbon.
BALLADS OF THE NORTH COUNTRIE.
Edited, with Introduction, by Graham R. Tomson.
SONGS AND POEMS OF THE SEA. Edited by Mrs. Sharp.
SONGS AND POEMS OF FAIRYLAND.
Selected by A. E. Waite.
SONGS OF THE GREAT DOMINION.
Edited by W. D. Lighthall, of Montreal.

NOW READY. Price $1.00.

12mo, Cloth Gilt, 433 pages and 31 Full-page Illustrations.

STANLEY AND AFRICA.

By the Author of "Life of General Gordon."

This volume will be found to be one of the most complete and graphic records of the career and adventures of the great explorer, and for those who wish to know the history of Stanley's life and the significance of what he has achieved, no better nor more interesting guide will be found than the present volume.

THE
EUROPEAN CONVERSATION BOOKS.

In Limp Cloth, for the Pocket. Price 40 Cents.

FRENCH.	ITALIAN.
SPANISH.	GERMAN (*shortly*).

Compact and practical. Arranged to permit direct and immediate reference. All dialogue or inquiries not absolutely essential excluded. A few hints given for the benefit of those unaccustomed to travel.

Cloth Covers, Price 40 cents each.

VERY SHORT STORIES AND VERSES FOR CHILDREN.
By Mrs. W. K. Clifford
LIFE STORIES OF FAMOUS CHILDREN.
By the Author of " Spenser for Children.'
UNCLE TOBY'S BIRTHDAY BOOK.
NATURAL HISTORY OF BIRDS, BEASTS, AND FISHES.
By John K. Leys, M.A.
FACTS ABOUT INFANT FEEDING AND MANAGEMENT.
By Dr. C. Stennett Redmond.
A CHRISTMAS CAROL. By Charles Dickens.
ELOCUTION. By T. R. Walton Pearson, M.A.

Books at $3.00 each.

Large Imperial 8vo. Coloured Illustrations.

LIFE AND EXPLORATIONS OF DR. LIVINGSTONE.
By J. S. Robertson.
ENGLAND UNDER VICTORIA. By Author of " Grace Darling."
LIFE AND TIMES OF GARIBALDI. By Howard Blackett.
STANLEY AND AFRICA. By the Author of " General Gordon."

Books at $2.50 each.

A MUSICIANS' BIRTHDAY BOOK. Crown 4to.
Edited by Eleonore D'Esterre-Keeling.
Padded Green Morocco, $5.00.

LIFE OF GENERAL GORDON. Royal 8vo.
By the Author of " Our Queen," etc.

BLACKIE'S LAYS OF THE HIGHLANDS AND ISLANDS.
Price $1.00.

CPSIA information can be obtained at www.ICGtesting.com
Printed in the USA
BVOW032308160513

320965BV00010B/197/P